CONSTRUCTED GROUND

THE MILLENNIUM GARDEN DESIGN COMPETITION

CONSTRUCTED GROUND

THE MILLENNIUM GARDEN DESIGN COMPETITION

CHARLES WALDHEIM

Published for the Chicago Department of Cultural Affairs
by the University of Illinois Press / Urbana and Chicago.

© 2001 by the Board of Trustees
of the University of Illinois

Library of Congress Cataloging-in-Publication Data
Waldheim, Charles.
Constructed ground : the millennium garden design competition /
Charles Waldheim.
p. cm.
ISBN 0-252-02695-0 (cloth : alk. paper)
ISBN 0-252-07001-1 (paper : alk. paper)
1. Gardens–Illinois–Chicago. 2. Urban landscape–Illinois–Chicago.
3. Gardens–Competitions–Illinois–Chicago. 4. Urban landscape
architecture–Competitions–Illinois–Chicago. I. Title.
SB466.U65C568   2001
712'.5'0977311–dc21   2001001003

CONTENTS

ACKNOWLEDGMENTS

The publication of *Constructed Ground* has been made possible by the generosity, hard work, and goodwill of many institutions and individuals. Thanks to Mayor Richard M. Daley and the Mayor's Office for their vision in championing the Millennium Park public-private partnership. Thanks to Richard H. Driehaus and the Richard H. Driehaus Foundation for generously funding the garden competition and the book. Thanks also to all the members of the Garden Committee and the Garden Jury for their efforts and especially for their courage in supporting a demanding and innovative garden. Thanks to John H. Bryan for his leadership and fundraising activities for Millennium Park, and for serving as chairman of the Garden Committee.

This publication, and the competition it describes, would not have been possible without the work of Ed Uhlir, Director of The Millennium Park Project. Ed has been a constant source of inspiration, persisting with genuine humility to achieve significant cultural gains for Chicago. The book has benefited greatly from the efforts of the entire Millennium Park staff, Karen Durante especially. Equally invaluable have been the support and resources of the Chicago Department of Cultural Affairs, and Commissioner Lois Weisberg. Valentine Judge, Director of Marketing for Cultural Affairs saw the potential in the project, and put the talent and material in place, while steering the book's development toward an ambitious deadline. Cultural Affairs Programming Associate Angela Mendez pulled all the pieces together seamlessly from across three continents.

The Hennessy Design Group, Inc. is deserving of special mention for contributing inspired and intelligent design work. Thanks to Clare Hennessy for her fine eye and wonderful talents. Clare, Christie Lewis, Bryn Doherty and Laura Steur of Hennessy Design Group designed the book and are responsible for its rich visual quality.

Thanks to Judith Russi Kirshner, Dean of the College of Architecture and the Arts at the University of Illinois at Chicago, for creating a wonderfully supportive environment in which to work and for indulging my interest in landscape. Thanks also to Katerina Ruedi, Director of the School of Architecture at UIC for her optimism and encouragement, and to Xavier Vendrell, Professor of Architecture at UIC, for his insights into the jury deliberations and finer points of the project. Willis Regier, Director of the University of Illinois Press, contributed enormously with faith and consistent good humor at numerous milestones along an improbably tight timeline. Kate Reid impressed again with her acumen and stamina through the tedium of copyediting.

Of course the publication is deeply indebted to Kathryn Gustafson, Piet Oudolf, Robert Israel, and the entire design team of *The Shoulder Garden*. Without their remarkable alliance and extraordinary talents, Chicago would be much the poorer, having missed an opportunity to build a landscape truly worthy of the contemporary city. Finally, thanks to all the competitors, collaborators, and assistants who worked on the Millennium Garden Design Competition. Their efforts, while largely unheralded and unbuilt, ennoble our own and make ever more precious the prospect of building the one that won.

The publication of *Constructed Ground* has been generously supported by the Richard H. Driehaus Foundation, Sara Lee Corporation, Georgia-Pacific Corporation, Millennium Park Incorporated, and the Chicago Department of Cultural Affairs.

CHARLES WALDHEIM

DEDICATIONS

"I am pleased to congratulate Gustafson Partners, Ltd. along with Piet Oudolf and Robert Israel on winning Chicago's Millennium Garden Design Competition funded by Richard H. Driehaus. This thoroughly contemporary garden will not only provide space for gathering, but also a quiet retreat for contemplation and relaxation. It will become familiar to residents and to millions of tourists who visit each year as a spectacular example of city beautification that celebrates the spirit of the new millennium in Chicago."

RICHARD M. DALEY, MAYOR
CITY OF CHICAGO

"The Millennium Garden Design Competition has been a deeply creative process. It has allowed us to select an innovative and site-specific design by a team of world-renowned designers to complement the other major elements in Chicago's new front yard. I am happy to have contributed to this historic redesign of an American city's landscape."

RICHARD H. DRIEHAUS, PRESIDENT
THE RICHARD H. DRIEHAUS FOUNDATION

"The award-winning team of landscape architect Kathryn Gustafson, Dutch planting expert Piet Oudolf, and theatrical producer Robert Israel will create a wonderful new destination garden for Chicago. Thanks to the vision of Mayor Daley, and the generosity of Chicago's leading families, foundations, and corporations, Millennium Park will be one of the most remarkable urban spaces ever created in America. The Park will be Chicago's signature to the world and an abiding testament to one of the most noteworthy public-private partnerships of the century."

JOHN H. BRYAN, CHAIRMAN SARA LEE CORPORATION
CO-CHAIR MILLENNIUM PARK, INC.

Fig. 1. Oudolf Planting: Light Plate. Fig. 2. Israel Performance.
Fig. 3. Gustafson Landscape: Esso Headquarters.

FOREWORD

JUDITH RUSSI KIRSHNER

DEAN
COLLEGE OF ARCHITECTURE AND THE ARTS
THE UNIVERSITY OF ILLINOIS AT CHICAGO

Rarely has an established metropolis created an opportunity to represent itself as a cultural and civic center on what is arguably the most prominent site in its urban landscape. When the city of Chicago made the unprecedented decision to recast and dedicate the northwest corner of Grant Park to recreational activities, monumental sculpture, and performance, the challenge was enormous and explicit. The imaginative conclusion to the project, which itself has evolved into a fascinating collage of architectural and artistic conjunctions, has been led by John H. Bryan in the private sector and ably coordinated by Ed Uhlir of the Mayor's Office. The competition to create a destination garden and its publication here have been generously supported by Richard H. Driehaus and the Richard H. Driehaus Foundation. Once again the central intersections of commercial and cultural activity will be layered on a grand public scale along Lake Michigan.

The layering of political and social history, powerfully signified by the Art Institute's unique location spanning the railroad system, continues through dismantling and reassembling processes in functional and metaphorical reversals. The classically inspired peristyle first erected in the twenties will be rebuilt adjacent to a modernist giant, an abstract sculpture by British artist Anish Kapoor. Theaters are being excavated below grade, Spanish artist Jaume Plensa's glass towers serve as fountains, and a diagonal walkway, reflective steel wall, and watercourse will illuminate gardens on the ground of the new *Shoulder Garden*.

These fluid elements of *The Shoulder Garden* are emblematic of the stunning, serene design by Kathryn Gustafson Partners with plant specialist Piet Oudolf and lighting designer Robert Israel. *The Shoulder Garden* activates the contrasts of the twenty-four acre setting destabilizing its topography to push the notion of urban landscape to the reality of a fantastic mental map. Gustafson's work reflects the lessons of contemporary art's revolutionary earthworks of the late sixties and seventies, foregrounding the user's experience as constitutive to the meaning of the sculptural work, whose materials need not be limited to the studio, but fuse ecological systems with the drama of Chicago's changing seasons. Referring to the city's strength as cultural signifier, *The Shoulder Garden* heaves itself up from Monroe Street, inviting walkers to follow the wooden path between dark and light gardens, between sun and shade over shallow water. Strolling on the diagonal deck between the dynamic Frank Gehry Music Pavilion and the new northern face of the Art Institute, viewers are performers entering and exiting the bandshell lawn. As participants in a visual exercise, they can peer through the windows perforating the volumetric hedges and can physically engage the serene spaces and expansive garden vistas. What could have been another piece of a planning puzzle becomes the keystone of multiple readings of urban landscape design. Neither garden nor park, neither earthwork nor architecture, this environment thrusts itself into the visitor's experience as meeting place and promenade and collapses the separate disciplines of architecture, theatrical lighting, and planting into a brilliant interplay of natural conditions and cultural imperatives onto a monumental public stage.

Fig. 1. Oudolf Planting: Light Plate. Fig. 2. Gustafson Landscape: Shell Headquarters. Fig. 3. Israel Performance.

INTRODUCTION

The easy thing to forget about Chicago's lakefront park is that it almost never was. Chicago's most prized cultural inheritance, Grant Park, exists only as the result of countless hard-fought battles over the future of public space at the lakefront. Without that investment by generations of civic, political, and cultural leaders, Chicago's lakefront would doubtless be indistinguishable from the waterfronts of an endless list of second and third-tier towns and the vast majority of major metropolitan centers whose most valuable spatial asset was long ago lost to private ownership.

Initially formed in the nineteenth century as artificially constructed ground reclaimed from Lake Michigan, the lakefront's value was redoubled throughout the course of the twentieth century with the addition of now cherished buildings and landscapes, architectural monuments, and public art. Unfortunately, the last quarter of the twentieth century saw little improvement of those assets and rendered the original cultural investment vulnerable while the various cultural institutions and destination tourist sites of the lakefront continued to increase in popularity. This historical trend placed increasing demands on the infrastructure, landscape, and cultural amenities of Grant Park. During the past quarter century, enormous social transformations changed forever the way public landscapes are used, maintained, and financed while the nineteenth century design and twentieth century improvements of Grant Park could not possibly keep pace.

Like any inheritance, cultural capital can just as easily be lost to benign neglect through the accumulated effects of inflation on a static investment over time. In order to ensure the original cultural bequest might be available to future generations, a plan is required to guide future growth and accumulated interest must be intelligently re-invested. The Millennium Park Project will go a long way toward accomplishing those goals on the lakefront through the reconstruction of lost portions of historic Grant Park and the creation of twenty-four acres of newly constructed park ground atop new subsurface parking decks and the operating railroad tracks below. By converting what had been privately operated surface parking lots and railroad yards into a new public park, Millennium Park rejoins Chicago's ongoing battle against private ownership of the lakefront.

The landscape centerpiece to Millennium Park will be *The Shoulder Garden* designed by landscape architect Kathryn Gustafson, Dutch plant expert Piet Oudolf, and theatrical designer Robert Israel. Sited at the southeast corner of the new park, the garden will connect Frank Gehry's Music Pavilion to the north with the new Art Institute of Chicago addition by Renzo Piano to the south, forming a triumvirate of world-class cultural destinations. *The Shoulder Garden* will be an international caliber destination landscape to be experienced year round by generations of Chicagoans and tourists alike. An innovative and uncompromising design on an historic site, *The Shoulder Garden* will bring Chicago's lakefront squarely into the twenty-first century with the construction of contemporary landscape unlike anything built in North America to date.

Fig. 1. Oudolf Planting: Light Plate. Fig. 2. Israel Performance.
Fig. 3. Gustafson Landscape: Shell Headquarters.

CONSTRUCTING MILLENNIUM PARK

EDWARD UHLIR

DIRECTOR
MILLENNIUM PARK PROJECT

The opening of Millennium Park celebrates the new millennium with innovative public art projects, performance venues, and a stunning landscape. Completion of the project, slated for 2003, will represent the successful resolution of numerous challenges including issues of land ownership, finance, public participation, planning approvals, design coordination, construction management, and scheduling.

Located at the northwest corner of Grant Park, the site for Millennium Park includes an eight-acre historic edge along Michigan Avenue as well as a sixteen and a half-acre railroad terminal and parking lot twenty feet below the surrounding street elevation. Since this railroad property was believed to be inviolate, it remained as a void in both Burnham's 1909 Plan of Chicago and in Edward Bennett's subsequent 1922 design for Grant Park. In 1997, Mayor Richard M. Daley directed his staff to find a way to cover the unsightly tracks and parking lot with a new "state-of-the-art" music pavilion replacing the aging and functionally obsolete Petrillo Music Shell.

The railroad was persuaded to donate their rights, title, and interest in the property to allow the construction of a new park. A new parking garage was proposed that would ultimately pay for itself as well as the structure over the railroad tracks and the electrical, mechanical, and civil infrastructure for the new park. Tax Increment Financing and Metropolitan Pier and Exhibition Authority funds were dedicated to provide the city's funding for the basic park infrastructure, including soil, landscaping, paving, and lighting.

A private sector committee led by John H. Bryan was formed at the Mayor's request to underwrite park "enhancements" including public art, fountains, special architectural features, a new garden, and the music pavilion. This donor group has made significant progress toward the goal of $100 million for capital improvements and an additional $25 million for an endowment, of which a major portion will be used to maintain the new Millennium Garden.

The first design for the new garage and park, by Skidmore, Owings, and Merrill, was an extension of Edward Bennett's French *Beaux-Arts* plan for the rest of Grant Park. This design was significantly revised with the inclusion of a newly reconstructed North Underground Garage under a reconstructed portion of Grant Park,

Fig. 1. Oudolf Planting: Light Plate. Fig. 2. Gustafson Landscape: Esso Headquarters. Fig. 3. Israel Performance. Fig. 4. Aerial View Grant Park.

designed by Teng Associates. This redesign, along with subsequent donor support, led to the inclusion of the Chicago Music and Dance Theater and the commissioning of Frank O. Gehry Associates to design the Music Pavilion.

The Chicago Music and Dance Theater, designed by Hammond, Beeby, Rupert & Ainge, will sit underground behind the Music Pavilion proscenium and stage, largely covered with park landscape above. The inclusion of the firm of Frank O. Gehry Associates as designers of the Music Pavilion was made possible by a generous pledge of $15 million by the Pritzker Foundation. The sculptural exterior of the proscenium reflects Gehry's distinct style, wrapping the stage in a series of stainless steel curving panels that resemble the petals of a flower. The adjoining trellis forms a light structure in steel above the Great Lawn below. The audio system suspended from the trellis is the first of its kind for an outdoor venue and creates an "electronic architecture" by providing virtual walls and ceilings to this outdoor room.

The performance shell will accommodate a full-sized symphony orchestra and up to 150 choral members on an elevated terrace. The stage can be enclosed at the proscenium for weather protection and temperature control by full height mechanically operated glass doors, allowing year-round interior performances. A quick draining sand-based, reinforced turf system and integral irrigation and drainage systems will provide in excess of 6,000 comfortable lawn-seating positions. There will be 4,000 self-rising, contoured stadium-type seats positioned for excellent sight lines to the stage. A Gehry designed pedestrian bridge will connect Millennium Park with Grant Park to the east. This sinuous stainless steel structure will span Columbus Drive and will be gently sloped to minimize the effort required by people with disabilities.

Significant donor contributions have allowed several other elements to be included on each of three blocks along Michigan Avenue. Between Randolph and Washington Streets, the 1917 Edward Bennett designed peristyle will be reconstructed, announcing the northwest gateway to the park. The neo-classical design, razed in 1953 to make way for the first Grant Park underground garage, consists of a semicircular arrangement of paired Doric columns. This reconstructed landmark, designed by OWP&P Architects, as well as the surrounding commons area, is being made possible by the generosity of the William Wrigley Jr. Company Foundation.

Fig. 1. Millennium Park Site. Fig. 2. Millennium Park Construction.
Fig. 3. Millennium Park Master Plan.

Between Washington and Madison Streets, a new ice skating rink and activity plaza will be installed as a gift of the Robert R. McCormick Tribune Foundation. Included will be public restrooms, skate rental, and warming facilities. A 300-seat year-round restaurant will expand outdoors when the weather allows it. On the terrace above the skating rink, an extraordinary new work of public art by internationally known artist Anish Kapoor is made possible by a gift from the Ameritech Foundation. The seamless, highly reflective stainless steel sculpture measures 35 feet wide and 65 feet long and rises 28 feet high.

Between Madison and Monroe Streets, a year-round interactive fountain is planned. Currently being designed by Jaume Plensa of Barcelona, the proposed fountain features a constantly changing exhibition of electronic images, light and water. These elements, along with the Frank Gehry projects and the new addition to the Art Institute by Renzo Piano, form the context for the Millennium Garden Design Competition documented here.

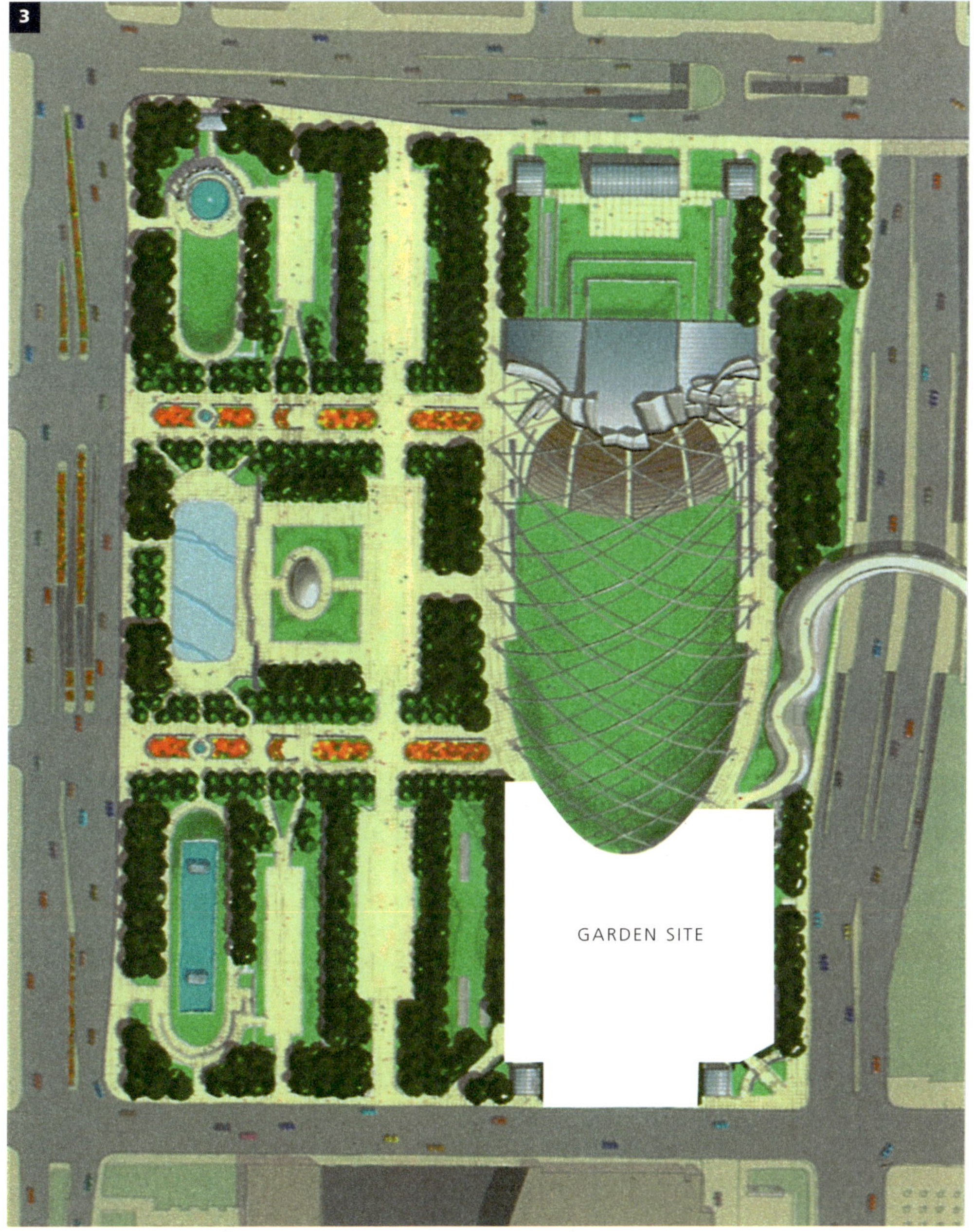

1
2
3

CHICAGO'S LAKEFRONT PARK

The fact Chicago's lakefront is an artificial construction rather than a naturally existing shoreline has made its ownership an historical difficulty of some import. The arbitrarily constructed and constantly shifting boundary between inland city and inland sea has been a consistent site of contention between public rights and private interests. Prior to the nineteenth century, what would become Chicago's eastern edge along Lake Michigan south of the Chicago River was a marshy flatland. The construction of Fort Dearborn at the mouth of the Chicago River in 1804 marked the site's strategic importance to the eventual colonization and development of the West.

By the time of Chicago's incorporation in 1837, twenty acres of federally owned Fort Dearborn lands had been set aside as open space. In 1844, the city took ownership of these lands which had been designated as "public ground forever to remain vacant of buildings." A portion of this land at the mouth of the river was acquired by the Illinois Central Railroad along with trackage rights extending south along the edge of lake, while the city maintained ownership of the land east of Michigan Avenue including the submerged land beyond the railroad right of way. Eventually Illinois Central was granted trackage rights for a new railroad trestle that was constructed offshore, while the city still maintained ownership of the submerged land on either side. By 1857, the area south of the Chicago River and north of Randolph Street had been filled with railroad terminals, yards, warehouses, and other industrial uses.

By the 1860's, economic and political pressure to devote the lakefront to industrial development reached its peak. In

Fig. 1. Oudolf Planting: Dark Plate. Fig. 2. Gustafson Landscape: Morbras Park. Fig. 3. Israel Performance. Fig. 4. Joshua Hathaway's Plat Map of Chicago 1834. Fig. 5. James Palmatary's View of Chicago 1857.

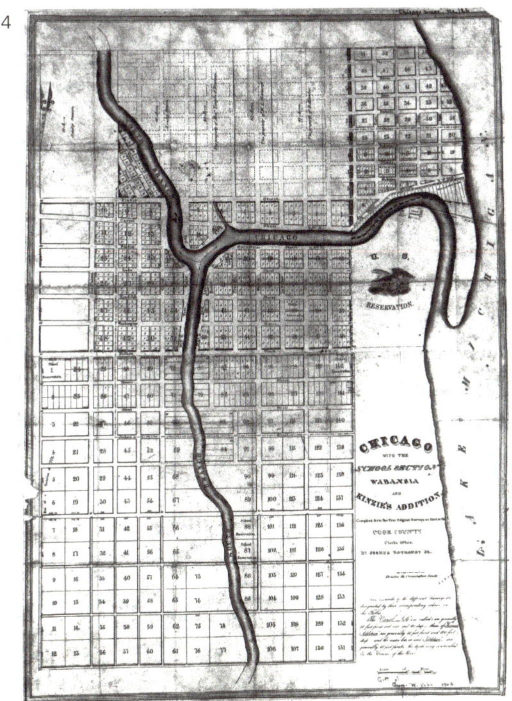

opposition to those sentiments, Chicagoans united around their rights to the lakefront and various court battles and legislative enactments consistently reiterated the public grounds east of Michigan Avenue, including the submerged lands east of the railroad, were open space not to be encroached upon by buildings. The 1870's and 1880's saw a steady increase in the 's boundaries through landfill, particularly following the Fire of 1871. A decade later, minimal landscape improvements were made to the western edge, which had been termed Lake along Michigan Avenue. In spite of these improvements and perennial court battles, the site continued to be used as a dumping ground and suffered the erection of numerous livery stables and squatters' shacks through the 1880's.

In 1890, A. Montgomery Ward filed suit demanding that the Park be cleared of structures. In response, Chicago ordered the removal of all unauthorized buildings in the park and solicited the first of what would be many lakefront plans for Chicago. By 1892, the United States Supreme Court finally concluded a series of lengthy legislative disputes and court battles with a decision against the state of Illinois granting all ownership of the lakefront south of Randolph Street and north of 11th Street, including submerged lands, to Chicago. This decision ratified the notion that the lakefront would remain open, free, and clear in perpetuity while acknowledging usage rights that allowed the railroad to continue operating.

In the wake of the decision, public interest in a proper plan for the lakefront intensified. Between 1895 and 1909 many competing lakefront proposals were published including, plans by Peter B. Wight, the Olmsted Brothers, and Daniel Burnham. Daniel Burnham and Edward Bennett's 1909 Plan for Chicago featured the Burnham designed Field Museum at the center of an axial organization of the site and relied on a formal vocabulary of *Beaux-Arts* architectural elements in the manner of the French *Ecoles*. Following another lawsuit resulting in the removal of the Field Museum to another location south of the park and Burnham's death, Edward Bennett was commissioned to execute a new plan for Grant Park in 1915. Between 1915 and 1922 planning and construction were pursued simultaneously beginning with the western edge of the park along Michigan Avenue. By 1922, Bennett and his partners published a comprehensive plan for Grant Park. While much of that project was constructed between 1925 and 1930, many of its elements were never executed and its plantings never completed. Among the monumentally scaled architectural elements completed were Buckingham Fountain, the park's centerpiece, and a semicircular colonnade of neo-classical columns, or peristyle, at the northwest corner of the site at Michigan Avenue and Randolph Streets, forming the Park's north gateway.

While portions of the park, including Buckingham Fountain, are listed today on the National Register of Historic Places, post-World War II development was more

Fig. 1. Michigan Avenue circa 1868-69. Fig. 2. Grant Park Parking Lot 1923. Fig. 3. View of Grant Park 1938. Fig. 4. Aerial View Millennium Park Site. Fig. 5. Lakefront Railroad Yard.

concerned with accommodating the automobile than maintaining the historic character of the site. In 1953, the North Underground Garage was completed at the cost of the demolition of the historic peristyle at the site's northwest corner and the removal of many trees. In 1961, the South Underground Garage was constructed, and in 1976, the Monroe Street parking replaced surface parking on the site. Those improvements notwithstanding, Grant Park continued to struggle to keep pace with the onslaught of the automobile and growing numbers of visitors. One remarkably constant feature of the park as constructed, as well as the various historical plans for its development, has been the presence of the historical railroad rights-of-way cutting through the park. While these railroad tracks, platforms, terminals, and yards were dropped below grade in the 1920's, they persisted as a visible scar across the city's front yard until 1998 when construction began on Millennium Park.

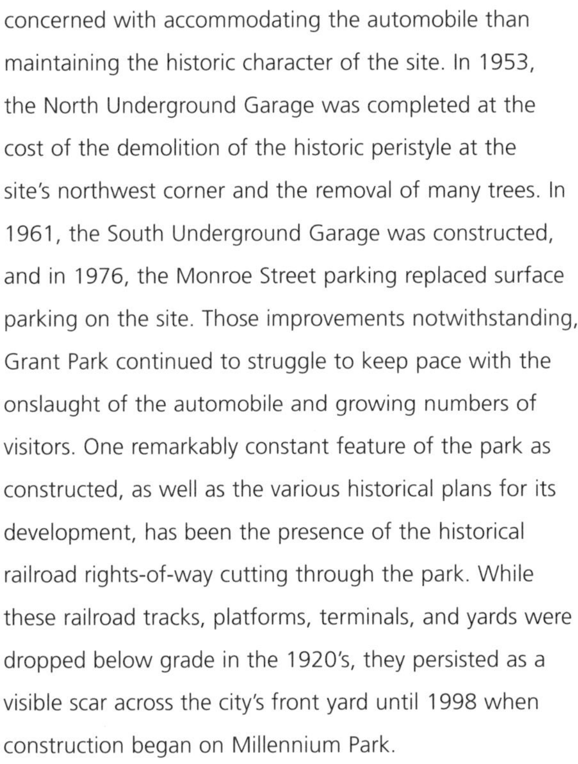

CULTURED GROUND

THE MILLENNIUM GARDEN

The Millennium Garden was conceived as the landscape centerpiece to Millennium Park and a destination cultural event in its own right. The site for the garden comprises a thinly spread four-foot layer of new soil across two and a half acres of new subterranean parking structure at the corner of Monroe Street and Columbus Drive. The garden will sit south of the new Frank Gehry designed Music Pavilion and north of the proposed Renzo Piano addition to the Art Institute. To the east, the new Frank Gehry designed bridge will connect Millennium Park to the rest of Grant Park and the lakefront beyond. To the west will sit the rest of Millennium Park's public art improvements, including the Anish Kapoor sculpture, proposed Jaume Plensa fountain, and the reconstructed neo-classical peristyle, replete with donor's names engraved in limestone.

Rather than considering the landscape construction of the park to be a financial liability, the Millennium Park Project stewards conceived of it as a cultural asset, expecting it will serve as a destination event that will ultimately draw additional visitors who will pay to park, eat, be entertained, and enlightened. This comes from a new conception of landscape, a conception in which landscape is aligned with infrastructure that supports it, both fiscally and physically. In this conception of landscape, cultural work is allied with public works and gardens form one element in a dense concentration of cultural attractors forming a single massive architectural construction. In this sense, Millennium Garden sits like a roof terrace above an enormous cultural and entertainment complex.

As on a roof terrace, multiple stairs and elevators connect the garden to the parking garage below. Additional subterranean connections include planned pedestrian tunnels to the south and east underneath the busy surface traffic on Monroe Street and Columbus Drive, respectively. Pedestrian pathways connect the garden to the new Great Lawn to the north and Millennium Terrace to the east. Adjacent are some of the most notable landscape commissions in Chicago's recent history. The north and south courtyards of the Art Institute were designed by the landscape architects Laurie Olin and Dan Kiley respectively, while the landscape of Grant Park, itself listed on the National Register of Historic Sites, is currently the subject

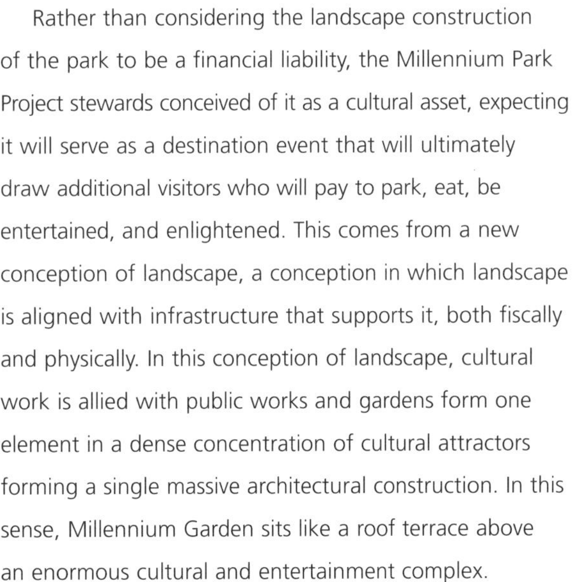

Fig. 1. Oudolf Planting: Light Plate. Fig. 2. Gustafson Landscape: Terrasson Park. Fig. 3. Israel Performance. Fig. 4. Aerial View Grant Park.

of a framework plan being executed by the office of George Hargreaves Associates Landscape Architects.

While virtually all other sites within Grant Park had been extensively documented and delineated by the founding fathers of Chicago lakefront patrimony, this oddly shaped wedge of land atop an underground parking garage that heaves itself up out of the lakefront was never designed. While nearly any debate surrounding the future of Chicago's lakefront can be traced back to original intent through a strict constructionist reading of the city's founding documents, neither founding father Burnham nor his plan can shed any light whatsoever on this little divot of sod. This is simply because it was never conceived to be anything more than an ugly absence in the otherwise seamless carpet of Chicago's lakefront.

The Garden Committee, as it came to be known, brought together Millennium Park Project Director Ed Uhlir, Millennium Park Co-Chair John H. Bryan, Richard H. Driehaus, and other notable Chicago civic and cultural leaders. This group settled upon a two-stage invited international design competition as the only vehicle worthy of this historic charge. Beginning with a long list of eighteen of the world's best landscape and garden design professionals and firms, the committee invited each to prepare initial designs for what would be a world-class destination garden for the new millennium. The competition brief described a laudable and high-minded set of goals for the project including the construction of a forward looking landscape design in the context of one of Chicago's most historic sites. The design needed to respond equally well under the extremes of Millennium Park's population, tens of thousands of visitors streaming to and from the major lakefront events contrasted with ten people on a quiet Sunday morning. The garden was to provide a contrast and complement to the scale and character of the expansive Grant Park. It was meant to provide a yearlong floral display, unique to the region and unparalleled in Chicago's existing botanical gardens, horticultural displays, and landscape institutions. The garden was meant to provide seasonal interest across the harshest of winters and busiest of summers.

Of the original eighteen entrants invited, five declined to participate, one entrant subsequently withdrew, and two entrants chose to collaborate as a team, to their mutual benefit and ultimate success. The resulting eleven projects were juried anonymously by an extraordinary jury of design professionals, civic leaders, and cultural critics including Gerard T. Donnelly, Executive Director of the Morton Arboretum; Posy Krehbiel, garden patron and enthusiast; Donna La Pietra, Executive Producer Kurtis

Fig. 1. Frank Gehry Music Pavilion and Pergola. Fig. 2. Frank Gehry Music Pavilion and Bridge. Fig. 3. Frank Gehry Music Pavilion Proscenium. Fig. 4. Anish Kapoor Sculpture.

Productions; Mike Lash, Director of Public Art, City of Chicago; Deborah Needleman, Editor at Large, *House and Garden Magazine;* Janet Meakin Poor, Director Chicago Botanic Garden; Adrian Smith, Senior Design Partner, Skidmore, Owings & Merrill; Maria Smithburg, Principal, Artemisia Landscape Architecture; Xavier Vendrell, Professor of Architecture, University of Illinois at Chicago; John Vinci, Principal Vinci/Hamp Architects; and James N. Wood, President, The Art Institute of Chicago. Ed Uhlir served Ex Officio and John H. Bryan chaired the jury.

Following the anonymous evaluation of the entries, this jury selected three projects for further development in the second stage of the competition: *Millennium Garden* by the Office of Dan Kiley, *Urban Riff Garden* by Jeff Mendoza Gardens; and *The Shoulder Garden* by the team of Kathryn Gustafson Partners with Piet Oudolf and Robert Israel. Landscape architect Gustafson and Dutch garden designer Oudolf, invited to compete independently, chose to form a team. The product of their collaboration with theatrical lighting designer Robert Israel was the unanimous selection of the competition jury as the project most deserving of construction.

THE SHOULDER GARDEN

The competition jury found *The Shoulder Garden* "bold, intellectual, daring, cutting-edge." In its unique combination of spatial structure, plantings, and lighting design *The Shoulder Garden* will be unlike any comparable landscape in North America.

The winning scheme clearly bears the mark of each of its three creators in distinct ways. Landscape architect Kathryn Gustafson is best known for her public landscapes and plazas in Europe where she has practiced extensively. Her interest in abstract form and clearly articulated spatial structure is evident in the overall organization of the garden and its spatial enclosure. Dutch plant expert Piet Oudolf brings his virtuoso horticultural expertise from an internationally recognized practice as a garden designer. His passion for texture, color, and grouping of plants is evident in the plant palettes of *The Shoulder Garden,* as well as the garden's seasonal transformations. Robert Israel brings an international reputation as a lighting designer for opera and theater. His contribution to *The Shoulder Garden* is evident in its lighting, day to night transformation, voyeuristic views, metaphorical naming devices, and narrative structure. Together, this team represents an improbable and enormously fortuitous professional liaison, a collaboration of individuals each internationally recognized in their area of expertise.

The Shoulder Garden, in addition to being the most fully developed and clearly articulated design submitted, was the only finalist project to move with equal confidence between the largest spatial structure of the site and the smaller scaled spaces of the plantings. As a result, the design works effectively with both the crushing presence of tens of thousands of concertgoers streaming out of the Music Pavilion toward Monroe Street, as with ten visitors on a Sunday morning. Perhaps most importantly to the jury deliberations, *The Shoulder Garden* offers a rich and varied sensory experience throughout the seasons with a complex layering of plant material, ground cover, and enclosure.

Fig. 1. Oudolf Planting: Light Plate. Fig. 2. Gustafson Landscape: L'Oreal Factory. Fig. 3. Israel Performance. Fig. 4. Shoulder Garden Site Diagram.

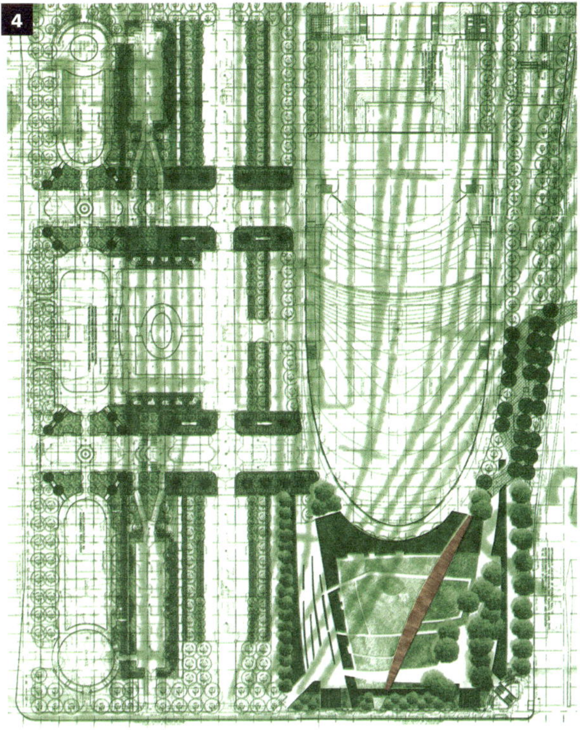

The only finalist project enhanced by the presence of visitors, *The Shoulder Garden* frames visitors as players in a drama of their own devising. Using dense hedgerows as backdrops, the garden invites the visitor to occupy its spaces in a series of sequential staged theatrical relationships. As in the theater, lighting forms a part of the narrative structure of the drama, with colored lights illuminating colored plants and creating an evening ambience that distinguishes the project by night and day, season to season.

The primary organizing device and spatial divider in the garden are a series of enormous sculpted waveform hedgerows. These hedges form dense impenetrable walls that enclose the garden on the north and west sides, protecting the heart of the garden from the massive crowds of the Music Pavilion. The northern leg of *The Shoulder Hedge* rests up against the Great Lawn of the Gehry Music Pavilion and its concave shape receives its geometry and sound. The western edge of the hedge helps to enclose the garden from *Extrusion Plaza* on the garden's western boundary.

The interior of the garden is cleaved into two planting areas of distinct character: *Light* and *Dark Plates.* Slightly tilted up to the south to benefit from the available sunlight and enhance its visibility from the new Art Institute addition, the two planting plates provide the spatial and thematic structure within which a complex array of plantings are layered based on their physical structure, textures, colors, and seasonal variation. The joint between the plates is rendered by *The Seam*, a wooden walkway over a water element extending diagonally from the northeast corner of the site where it connects with Frank Gehry's new pedestrian bridge to the lakefront. Cutting through the heart of the site to the southwest, *The Seam* traces the historical shoreline of Lake Michigan and the line of the railroad right of way below. This element of continuity between the Music Pavilion to the north and the Art Institute addition to the south serves as an archeological reference to the site's history in a contemporary design vocabulary.

The Shoulder Garden offers an absolutely world-class addition to Chicago's lakefront. In revealing the contemporary cultural conditions attendant to its inception, as well as the historical tensions evident in its formation, *The Shoulder Garden* moves well beyond simply physical beauty toward a genuine intelligence. By engaging visitors in a changing array of sensory perceptions over the seasons, the garden will quickly become a year-round destination as both horticultural event and prominent architectural site. By effectively connecting to its infrastructural underbelly, its star architect neighbors, and the larger framework of Millennium Park and Grant Park beyond, *The Shoulder Garden* reaffirms the increasingly important role of landscape as a mediating element in contemporary urban infrastructure. In the context of increasingly dense cultural attractors arrayed in close proximity to one another, *The Shoulder Garden* recommends itself as both a place to go and a way to get there.

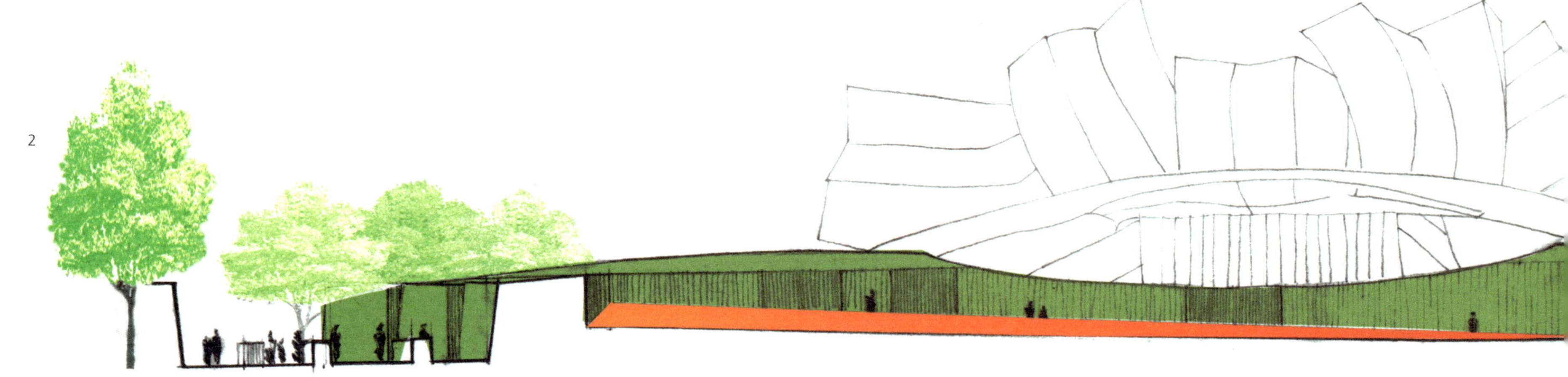

1
SOUTH PROMENADE 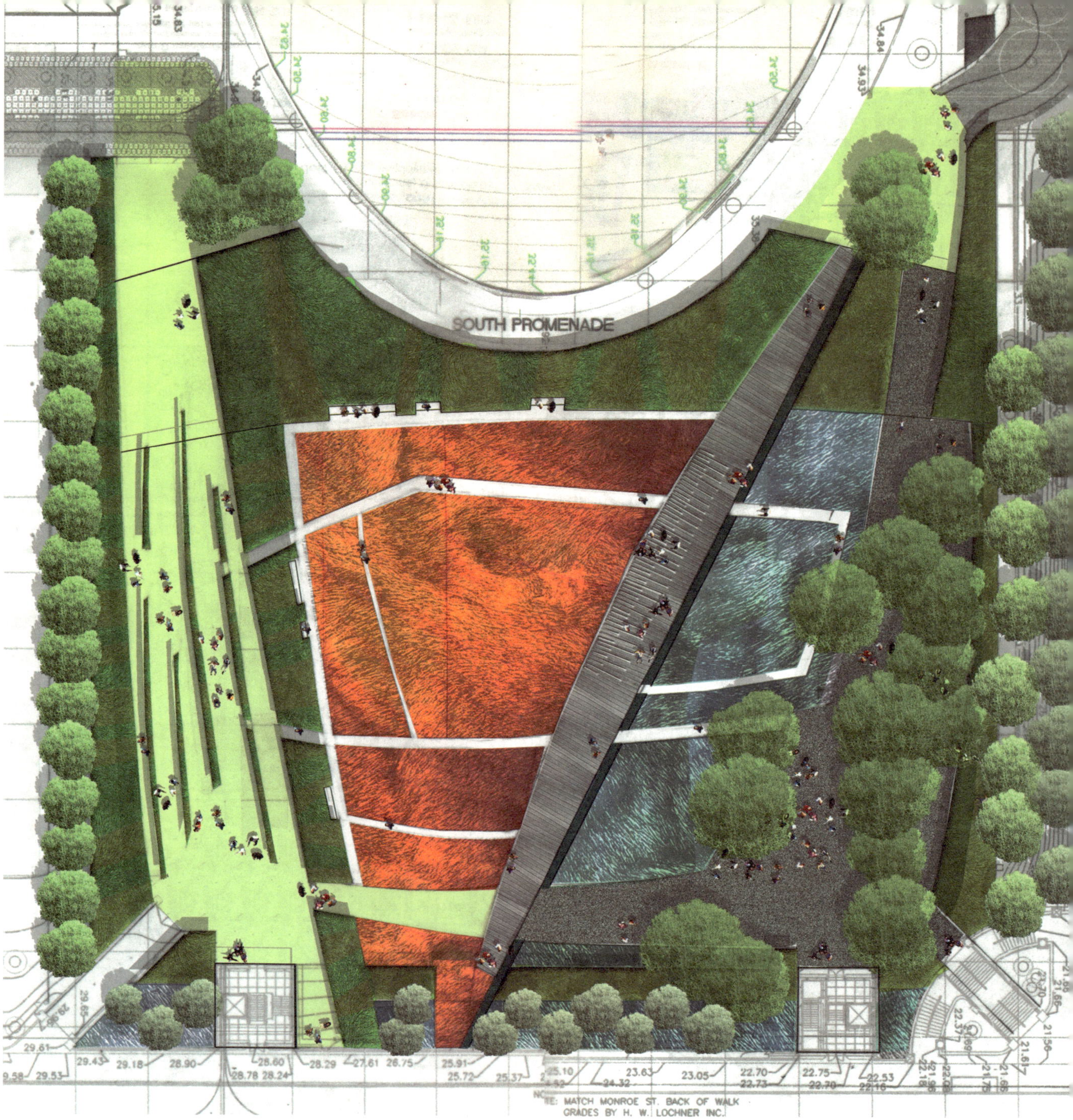
NOTE: MATCH MONROE ST. BACK OF WALK
GRADES BY H. W. LOCHNER INC.
2

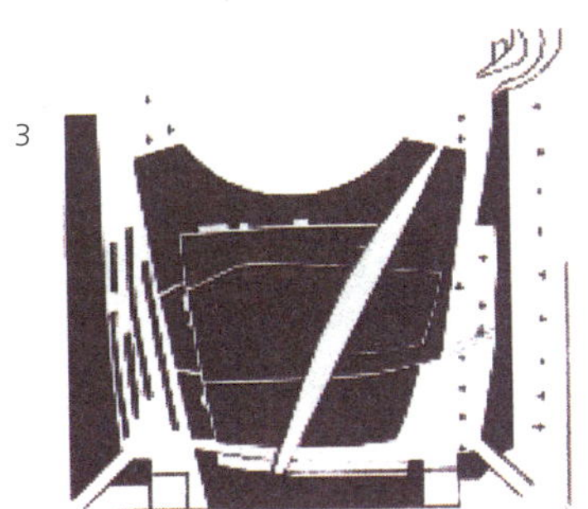

Planting

3

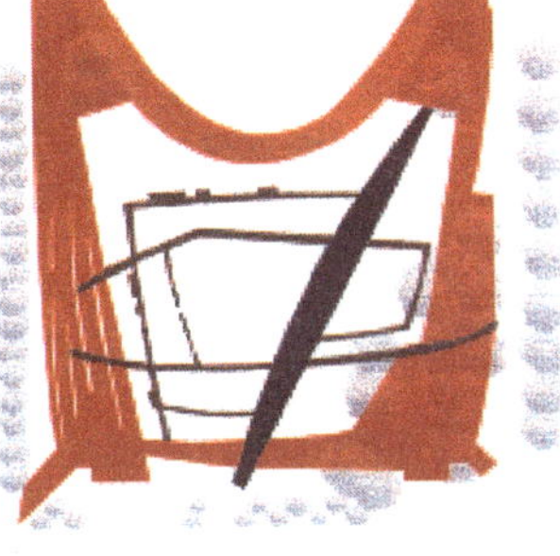

Circulation

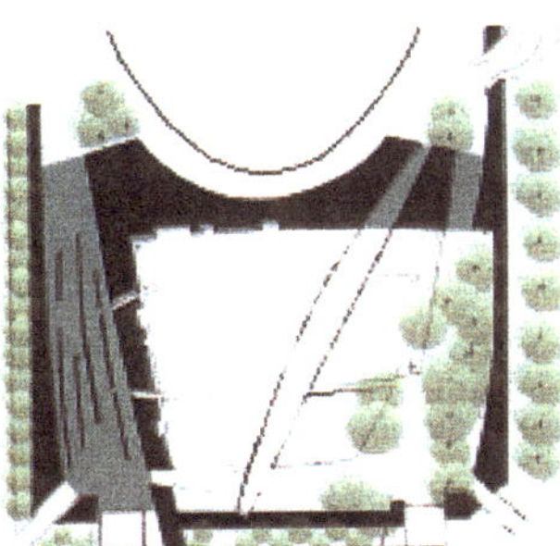

Enclosure

CONCEPT

KATHRYN GUSTAFSON

PIET OUDOLF

ROBERT ISRAEL

Chicago built itself out of marshy origins and continues to rise ambitiously upward. The site of the garden has been accordingly elevated from wild shoreline, to railroad yard, to roof garden. An increasingly refined control of nature and natural resources has accompanied Chicago's willful development. *The Shoulder Garden* celebrates the exciting contrast between the past and present that lay beneath and beside the site.

The strong grid layout of Chicago's streets highlights striking features that are not orthogonal. Such contrast is found in railways, which form sensuous braids that merge and swell. Angled roads radiate out of Chicago like crooked spokes from Grant Park's location in the center of the city. The paths and other forms of *The Shoulder Garden,* and their relationship to the formal grid structure of Grant Park, are inspired by these patterns and by the strong forms of Chicago's machines and architecture.

BIOGRAPHY

KATHRYN GUSTAFSON

Kathryn Gustafson's work emphasizes the sculptural qualities of site-specific and contextual landscape. She brings over twenty years of practice in landscape design, with her highly regarded work in France composing the majority of her previous work. In 1995, Gustafson began working throughout the European community and in the United States She presently practices with sister offices in Seattle and London.

Gustafson's projects have ranged in scale from one to 150 acres, in both urban and rural settings. Recent work includes the Arthur Ross Terrace in New York, the American Museum of Natural History, the Great Glass House at the National Botanic Garden of Wales, with Norman Foster, a fifteen hectare cultural park for the city of Amsterdam, the Seattle Civic Center, the Garden of Imagination in Terrasson, France, and the Seattle Performance Hall.

Gustafson is an honorary fellow of the Royal Institute of British Architecture, a medalist of the French Academy of Architecture, and the recipient of London's Jane Drew Prize. Gustafson is active in lecturing and her work has been published internationally.

Fig. 1. Garden Plan. Fig. 2. East-West Garden Section Looking North.
Fig. 3. Site Diagrams. Fig. 4. Color/Texture/Contrast Plant Collage.

THE SHOULDER HEDGE

A giant muscular hedge encloses the interior garden from the north and west. From the Art Institute's future addition, the "big shoulders" of *The Shoulder Hedge* appear to support the gleaming "headdress" of Gehry's music pavilion. *The Shoulder Hedge* creates a controlled interior landscape that looks toward the Art Institute and to the open sky over the Lake. *The Shoulder Hedge* creates an inhabitable backdrop to the interior garden with nooks that offer benches with commanding views.

INTERIOR PLATES

The interior of *The Shoulder Garden* is composed of two adjacent plates that appear "punched up" like metal panels from the surface of the plaza. The plates are dramatically contrasting, but together they resemble a muscular and armored torso.

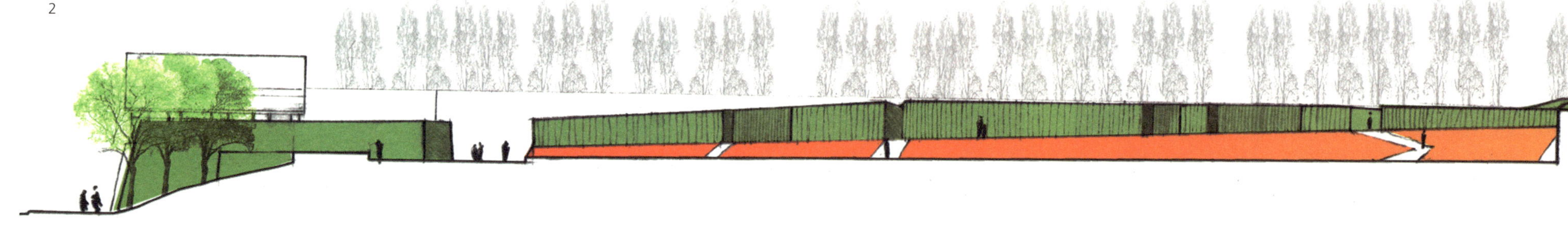

DARK PLATE

Strong, nostalgic, mysterious, and cool, *Dark Plate* expresses the intricate landscape history of the site and the city. The site was once a wild shoreline and river delta. The character and feeling of this historic condition dramatically contrasts the current elevation and form of Millennium Park. *Dark Plate* bursts with lush deep-toned vegetation that immerses the visitor in a setting of unbridled growth, exuberant textures, and soft filtered light. The deep tones and coarse textures of *Dark Plate* serve as a dramatically framed foreground to the smooth bright *Light Plate* on the other side.

The lush "rooms" of *Dark Plate* offer opportunities to sit in small groups facing the flow of people through *Meeting Grove*. Low canopies and strange plant effects form intriguing and adventurous spaces.

Like a breathing torso, *Dark Plate* rises with the absorption of warmth and light of the growing season. In the spring and summer, *Dark Plate* swells dramatically with robust shrubs and perennials. Intriguing, "primitive" shapes and colors emerge in foliage, flower, and fruit. In the fall, complexity reaches a crescendo, as fruit and foliage mature and the evergreen aspect of the plate begins to emerge as dominant. In the winter, the significant evergreen aspect of *Dark Plate* creates a landscape with new contours and spaces. Evergreen shrubs are positioned to playfully frame views and form special seating areas that are most dramatic.

BIOGRAPHY

PIET OUDOLF

Piet Oudolf is an internationally regarded plantsman, planting advisor, and detail-scale landscape designer. In addition to various projects for private gardens in Europe, he has worked on several public spaces and is involved in Rotterdam's Art Manifestation Project. Oudolf is also involved in the planting of the 2002 World Garden Exhibition *Floride* to be held in the Netherlands.

Oudolf's recent work includes a planting at the Botanical Garden Utrecht, the Enlioping Pocket Park in Sweden, a planting near the Maschsee in Hanover, and greenscape design of the new headquarters of ABN AMRO Bank in Amsterdam. He also developed the planting for Pensthorpe Waterfowl Trust in Norfolk, England. Oudolf's projects in the year 2000 included two large borders for the Royal Horticultural Society's Bicentennial Anniversary, the integration of public space into a hospital campus and the redesign of a public park in Rotterdam.

Oudolf's recent awards include winning Best-of-Show at the Chelsea Flower Show for *Gardens Illustrated* magazine. He recently published his fifth collaborative book on plants and planting.

Fig. 1. Perspective View Shoulder Hedge. Fig. 2. North-South Garden Section Looking West. Fig. 3. Shoulder Hedge. Fig. 4. Winter Character Plant Collage.

" *The Shoulder Garden,* a contemporary, site-specific design inspired by Chicago's distinct natural and cultural history, represents a fascinating opportunity and challenge. Juxtaposed between the downtown urban core, major cultural facilities, and the openness of Grant Park and Lake Michigan, the site will be experienced while strolling across the fantastic pedestrian bridge by Frank Gehry, as well as from the new addition to the Art Institute of Chicago by Renzo Piano. These connected public experiences demonstrate that Chicago is once again composing a statement of its leading role in contemporary art and architecture."

KATHRYN GUSTAFSON

" I have a reputation as an innovative garden designer based on my work with plants and a spontaneous way of planting. This spontaneity is due to the fact that we integrate plants with a wilder look and more naturalistic character. The use of ornamental grasses makes these plantings look different from traditional ones. Complemented by trees, hedges, and in harmonious balance with the spatial design of the garden, these plantings provide year-round interest. In that sense, Gustafson Partners and Robert Israel are the perfect colleagues for this unique project."

PIET OUDOLF

" I have always been interested in cross-disciplinary activities. As a collaborator, I feel at home working as a consultant to a large computer corporation, on the creative teams of two architectural firms, on the educational staff of a major museum, as an opera set and costume designer, as the Chairman of the Theater Department at UCLA, as a sculptor, as a teacher, and graphic designer. I look forward to this exciting collaboration. Hopefully, we will all bring to this wonderful opportunity a freshness that will produce something truly exceptional."

ROBERT ISRAEL

LIGHT PLATE

Rising, intellectual, abstract, and sublime, *Light Plate* renders the future in an exhilarating landscape. It is open, bold, warm, dry, and dazzlingly bright. From a distance, the large tilted planting is shimmering and perfect as an expression of human synthesis and abstraction. However, natural patterns and movements reveal themselves as one nears the plate and explores its fine-textured botanical complexity. Climbing the path to the high point of *Light Plate* rewards the visitor with empowering reflective views of the whole garden. This position provides an opportunity to appreciate the past and its challenges from the position of an inspired high point.

In the spring and summer, the colors of *Light Plate* radiate through a changing gradient of saturated brights. The careful orchestration of color progression renders *Light Plate* a visual calendar evident, from the Art Institute, from photographs, and from daily morning walks. In the winter, engaging textures bring detailed interest to a walk through the garden.

MEETING GROVE

Many visitors enter *The Shoulder Garden* from the stairs at the southeast corner. The first view from the top of the stairs is a dramatic invitation to the garden. Trees arch over the entry, framing a view in the welcoming "room" formed by the cool canopy of *Meeting Grove*. The shaded trunks frame views of stunning contrast toward the open sunlit landscape on the opposite side of the garden. Benches face the entry stairs to facilitate an easy meeting place for groups during busy event times.

BIOGRAPHY

ROBERT ISRAEL

Robert Israel has been designing theater and opera internationally for the past 28 years. His credits include the Paris Opera, the National Theater in London, the Vienna Statsoper, and the Metropolitan Opera in New York. He has designed the world premiers of four operas by Philip Glass. He is currently working in Austria, France, and the United States.

Israel is a member of the American Academy of Arts and Sciences, a Guggenheim recipient, and a former chairman of the Theater Department at UCLA. He continues at UCLA as a professor, working with the departments of music, theater, and architecture, as well as with researchers in plasma physics and the Brain-Mapping Center at the University.

Being a man of the theater, Israel brings an involvement in metaphor, scale, and illusion to his cross-disciplinary interests. He likes to think of himself as an audience member, participant, illusionist, and conscience of ambiguity.

Fig. 1. Night View Dark Plate and Meeting Grove. Fig. 2. Day View Dark Plate and Meeting Grove. Fig. 3. Sectional Perspective Meeting Grove. Fig. 4. Dark Plate and Meeting Grove Plant Collage.

Gustafson, Oudolf, and Israel bring together diverse and complementary skills of artistic expression and scale. Gustafson Partners' Seattle office will lead in the design development, working closely with Piet Oudolf to integrate his deep knowledge and interest in the beauty and emotional quality of plants in the landscape. With the guidance of Robert Israel's conceptual integrity, the exciting thematic and metaphorical qualities of the schematic design will be maintained through every aspect of the project.

EXTRUSION PLAZA

Hedges in machined shapes appear extruded from the smooth limestone paving of *Extrusion Plaza*. The hedges are arranged in a composition inspired by the movement patterns of goods in Chicago's rail yards. As people walk through the sculpted passages created by the hedges, they can watch each other move in organized patterns, as packets of information through the landscape. They can also catch glimpses of the colorful garden interior through whimsical windows in *The Shoulder Hedge*.

1

THE SEAM

The past and the future of Chicago are often placed as confident neighbors whose respective powers remain potent adjacent to opposites. *The Seam* is where the past and future meet face-to-face on either side of the visitor. *The Seam* is composed of a wall, a wood platform, and water. The linear wall, the edge of the raised *Dark Plate*, appears to have been pushed up by a force under the surface. The wall reflects the angle of railways under the site and suggests a surface reaction to their hidden energy. The wall creates a directional backdrop to the sweeping interior of *Light Plate*.

A wood platform, with occasional glimpses of water between the slats, follows the wall, as does a shallow channel of open water. These elements recall Chicago's first step at building itself out of the muddy landscape. As if walking on a timeline, a typical visitor will enter the garden through the mysterious, wild "past" of *Dark Plate* and enter the dry elevated "future" of *Light Plate* only by crossing the achievement of this platform. The platform swells at the center of the garden to allow visitors to congregate, stop, and sit.

Fig. 1. Axonometric Drawing. Fig. 2. Sectional Perspective
The Seam. Fig. 3. Perspective View Light Plate and Hedge Nooks.
Fig. 4. Light Plate Plant Collage.

THE FINALISTS

With his *Millennium Park Garden*, Dan Kiley, one of the most important landscape designers of the twentieth century, reprised his previous project for the Art Institute's south courtyard. Convinced what worked there and then will work equally well here and now, Kiley proposed a calm serene space of contemplation in the midst of a formally ordered and axially aligned *allée* of Hawthorn trees. The Hawthorns straddle a central watercourse aligned with the Music Pavilion to the north and cascading down a water stair at the south end of the site. The outer flanks of the site are protected with densely planted Hornbeam hedges while the terminus of the Great Lawn to the north is formed with a collar of London Plane Trees. With few exceptions, Kiley's scheme is absolutely bereft of flowering plants, and is sedate to the point of sedation. At times indistinguishable from the less well-maintained trees and lawns of Grant Park beyond, it remains unclear how the project contrasts with the remainder of the city's lakefront landscape. Kiley's project, while clearly representing the mature work of one of the discipline's modernist masters, fails to provide compelling evidence that it breaks new ground in contemporary landscape design. The garden's virtual lack of seasonal floral displays raises the question whether the Kiley scheme would be equally compelling as a destination throughout the year. Equally troubling is the scheme's rather rigid spatial structure and circulation in the face of the various avenues of approach from the Gehry bridge to the northeast, Millennium Terrace to the northwest, and the Art Institute to the south. Ultimately, while a purported virtue of Kiley's work is its timeless modern character, that very timelessness tends today to be a liability rather than an asset as it uncritically continues an understanding of landscape that purported to great insight a quarter century ago, failing to account for the changing conditions of contemporary culture.

Urban Riff Garden by New York's Jeff Mendoza invokes jazz improvisation as a metaphorical explanation for his device of a grid structure cut across by a sinuous curvilinear element. Intended to represent the various cultural, racial, and ethnic constituencies in the city of Chicago, Mendoza's garden is formed by two-dimensional planting beds interrupted by a serpentine glass wall. The resulting patchwork of planting sites is further distinguished by being viewed through the glass wall at various times of day, colors of glass, and lighting conditions. The curving glass wall has the spatial effect of rendering an inside and outside surface to alternate curves and thereby further differentiates the simplistic spatial structure of the grid. A pair of educational kiosks dispense plant information, while the obligatory water element negotiates the grade change to the south at Monroe Street. The jury praised Mendoza's rich diversity of plant palette, color, and theme as well as his innovative experiments with glass walls in relation to plants. Ultimately, however, the design is overly two-dimensional in its sectional relationship to the Music Pavilion and its connection to the site's circulation. The glass wall, while innovative, seems unresolved as a spatial organizer for the site. The general lack of spatial hierarchy contributes to confusion regarding the project's clarity of circulation and sequence. While certainly a destination garden with year round plantings of enormous interest, and an interesting innovation in glass vitrines for exterior plantings, the larger spatial and circulatory weaknesses of the project consigned it to be a clear runner-up.

Fig. 1. Oudolf Planting: Spring.
Fig. 2. Gustafson Landscape: Laussane Park.
Fig. 3. Israel Performance.

OFFICE OF DAN KILEY
MILLENNIUM GARDEN

IN CONTRAST TO the festive atmosphere of the Millennium Park master plan, the grand statement of Gehry's Music Pavilion and Great Lawn, *Millennium Garden* is a quiet composition with strength lying in its simplicity, purity, and harmony.

A thin crisp line of water and strong *allée* of trees issuing forth from the great expanse of lawn below Gehry's skeletal structure terminating in a serene cascade of water descending to Monroe Street reflects the new museum addition directly opposite. Broad planes of lawn panels or *tapis verte* flank this central spine sharpening the clarity and measure of the axis, while perimeter plantings of various height and form create a strong framework for the central garden and reach out to embrace the outlying elements of the garden precinct.

> The compact branching, bright gentle green leaves of the delicate tracery of the branching soften the formality of alignment without depleting the strength of the lines.

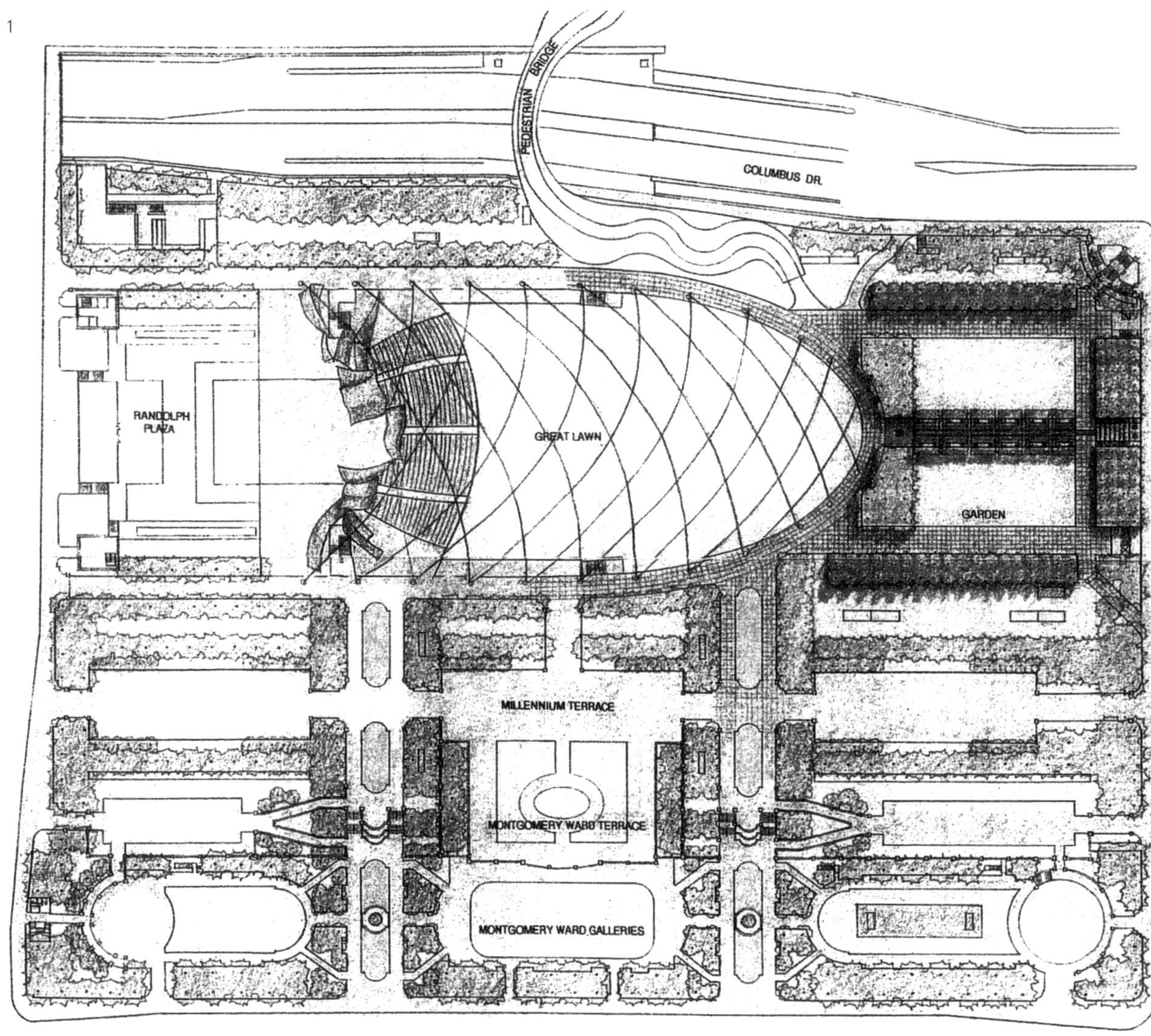

1

2

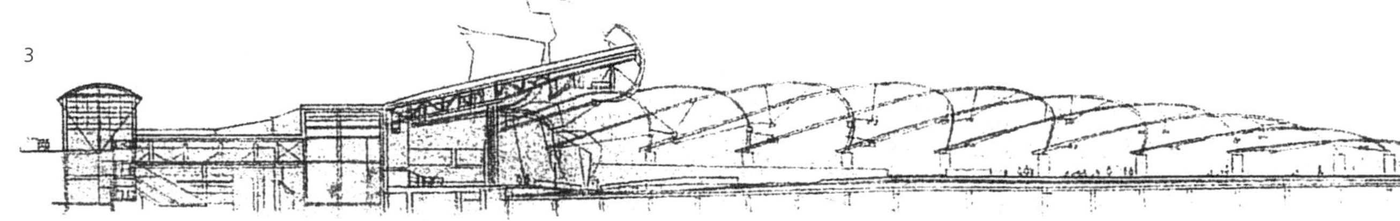

3

Tall double rows of Hornbeam hedges, with vinca below, create strong impenetrable edges on the east and west of the garden, screening mechanical units on the outer edges and focusing attention inward lending scale to the garden. The compact branching and bright gentle green leaves of the delicate tracery of the branching soften the formality of alignment without depleting the strength of the lines. Broad generous walks or promenades with lights and benches circulate the garden and Music Pavilion providing ample space for vast numbers of people. The broad openness of these walks contrasts and balances the intimately scaled central walkway along the canal.

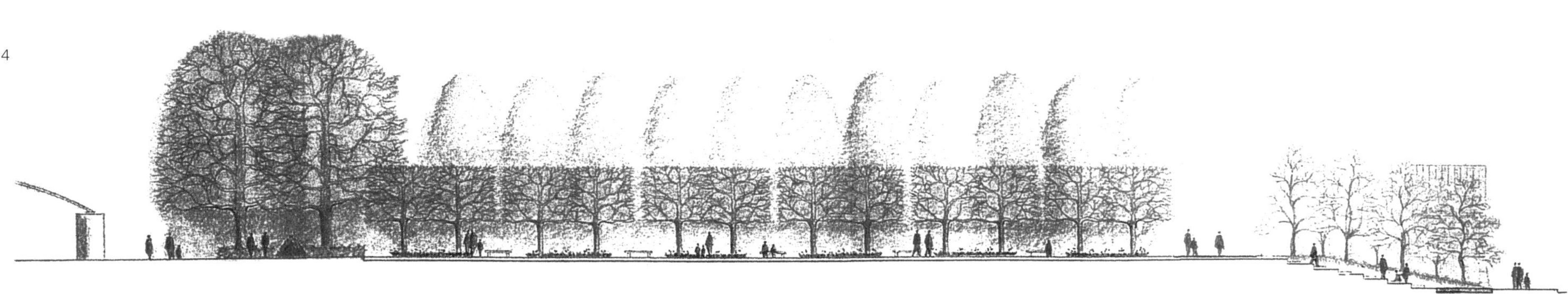

At the north end of the garden two groves of London Plane trees flank the entry to the canal-walk, gently curving on the North in acceptance of the Gehry Pavilion embracing the end of the great lawn. The inner edge of the grove, a crisp straight line, reinforces the geometry of the central garden panels. This end of the garden plays a critical role in wedding the grand scale of the Music Pavilion and Great Lawn with the more humble proportions of the garden space.

The heart of the garden is the central spine on axis with the Music Pavilion and the museum addition. A simple pure line drawn through the verdant lawn panels explodes dramatically into the Great Lawn to the north and then quietly flows down to the south. The simplicity and purity of design both compliment and augment the surrounding gardens and pavilion in a strong, yet understated way.

Fig. 1. Millennium Park Site Plan. Fig. 2. Perspective View from Monroe Street. Fig. 3. North-South Site Section. Fig. 4. North-South Garden Section. Fig. 5. Garden Plan.

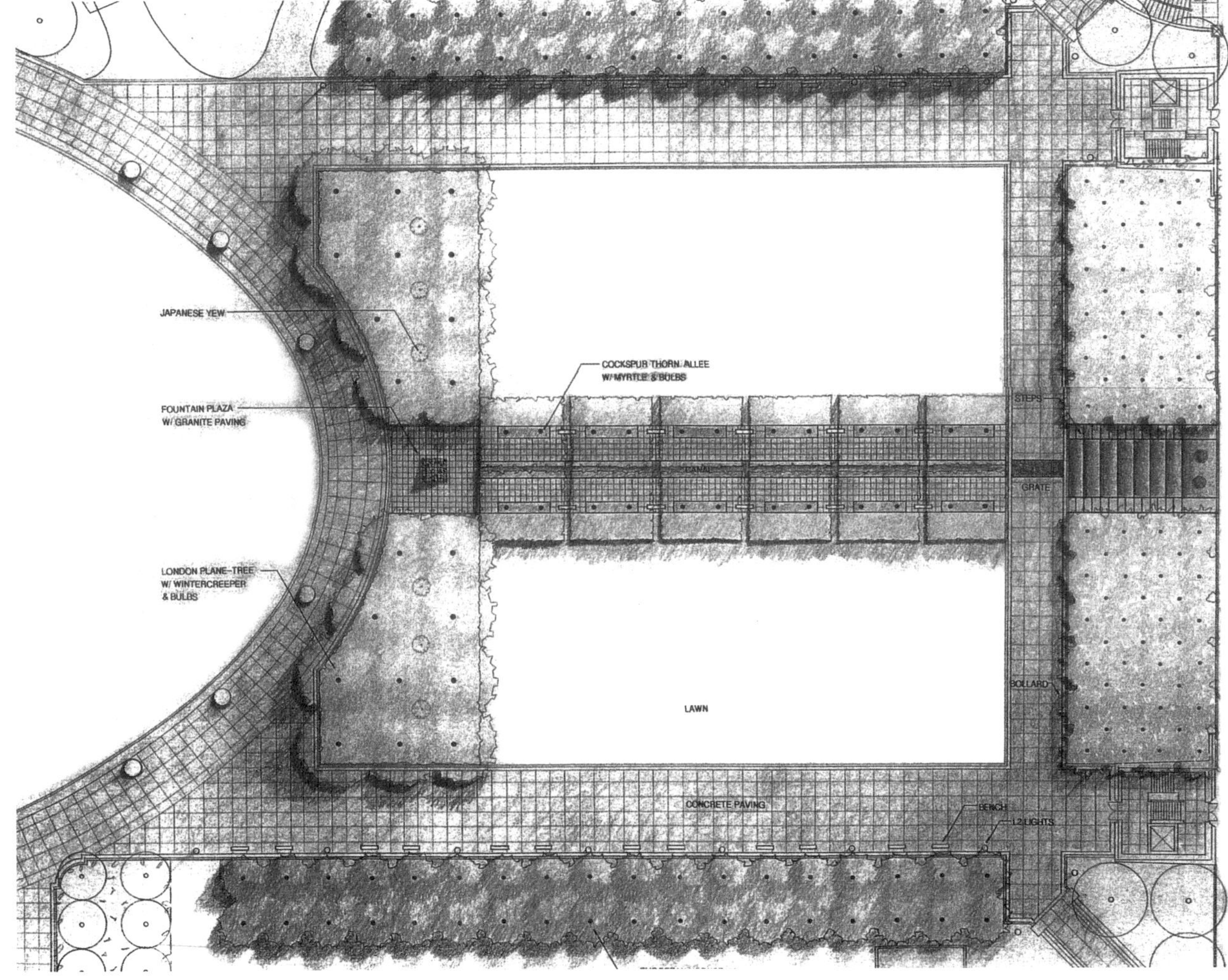

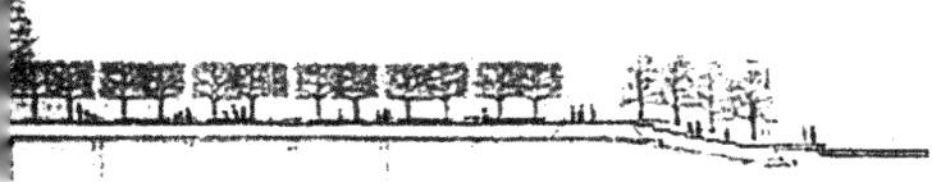

THE UNDERLYING FRAMEWORK of the garden is a grid. The grid operates not just as an image of urban form, a metaphor for order, but also as an embedded reference to the vision of Chicago's founders. The grid remains the dominant organizing pattern of Chicago and will address the contemporary programmatic need for physical and visual connectivity in the garden.

Today, Chicago's grid substructure is an orchestration of neighborhoods that are distinct yet interwoven to create a complex harmony. The membranes encompassing neighborhoods are both infrastructure systems and natural forms of the lake, river, and canals. The garden plan plays on this idea, providing a simple hierarchic structure as it weaves a complex harmony of plants and people.

> The grid remains the dominant organizing pattern of Chicago and will address the contemporary programmatic need for physical and visual connectivity in the garden.

1

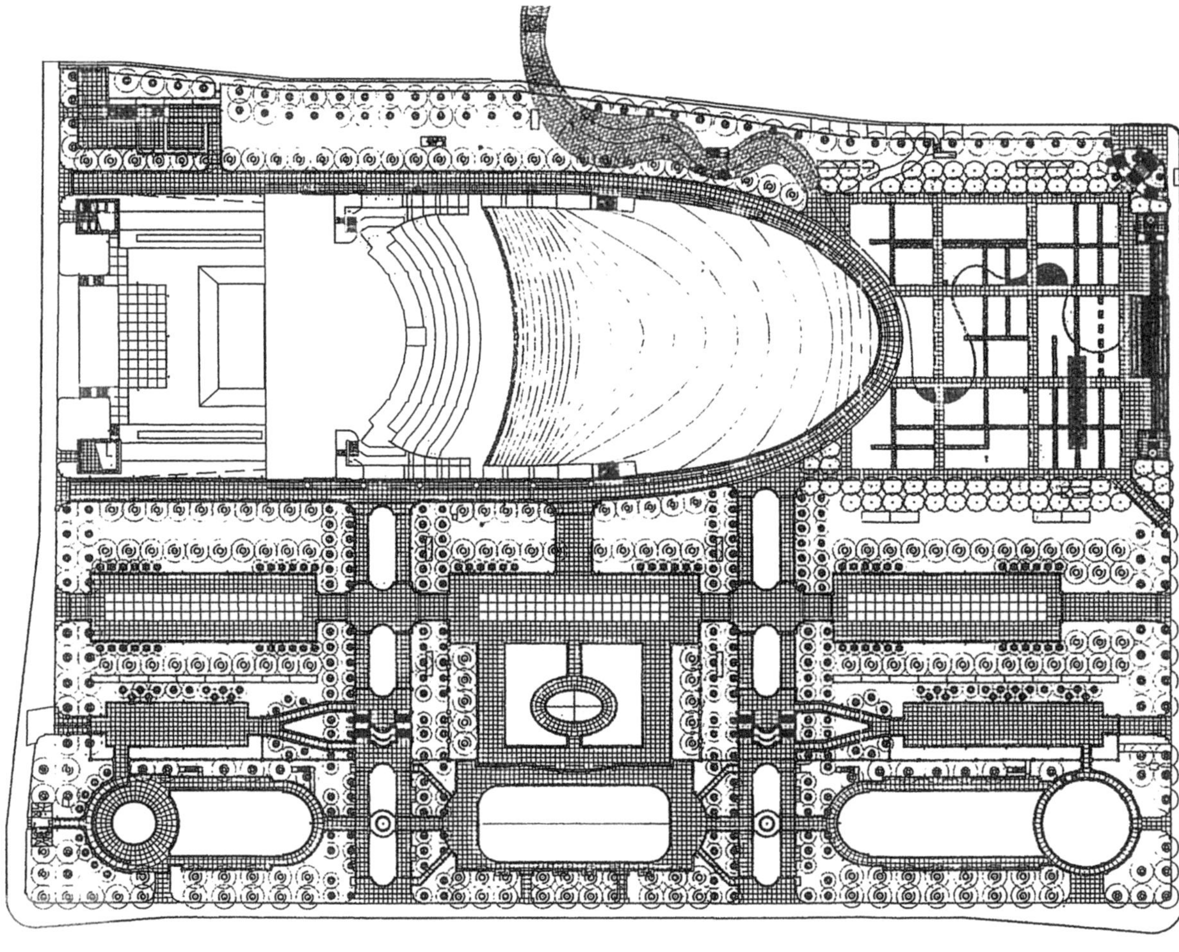

2

3

Millennium Park will be an overture to large-scale events and circulation for tens of thousands of visitors to be accommodated within the garden. It will also provide opportunities for intimate horticultural study as well as a refuge from which to escape or observe the rhythm of the city. Just as the various neighborhoods of Chicago reveal its character, so too the garden's numerous color-themed beds provide distinction and progression. The sequencing of form, texture, and color will be meticulously crafted to enunciate each phrase.

Proposed plantings are complex and richly textured, offering a symphony of color through spring, summer, and fall. The plant beds are composed of deciduous and evergreen trees, shrubs, herbaceous plants, bulbs, vines, annuals, and biennials. Deciduous and evergreen hedges syncopate the fields of herbaceous plants and pauses of

lawn provide punctuation within the garden. Architectonic evergreen hedges, filigrees of branches, and the dynamic effect of winter light on intervals of glass create a garden as mesmerizing in winter as in summer.

Like the river in the city, the glass meanders through the garden, a sinuous form intersecting, interrupting, and always altering the spaces it crosses. The glass elements are a shifting and discreet yet powerful presence in the landscape. The glass recalls the aqueous nature of the site originally and is evocative of the negotiation between the city and the river through history. The glass elements are of changing hue, texture, and luminosity. The modulated glass elements will visually transform both individual plants and compositions, suggesting a spectrum of landscape images from Monet's Impressionist paintings to the clarity of an elegant Ellsworth Kelly plant portrait. Sequences of pylons, bollards, and frameless glass walls modulate the viewing of plants both in detail and at a distance.

Fig. 1. Millennium Park Site Plan. Fig. 2. Perspective View Winter.
Fig. 3. East-West Garden Section. Fig. 4. North-South Garden Section.
Fig. 5. Garden Plan.

THE COMPETITORS

Notable among the competing projects eliminated in the first round was an entry by French landscape designer Louis Benech. Benech proposed a prairie field cut through with a series of narrow gravel pathways forming an enormous celestial chart in plan. These paths alternate with a grass field perceived from a distance to form a continuous prairie surface. Equally interesting in the prairie genre was Peter Walker's project for a prairie grass mound bisected axially by pairs of glass walls. From a central pathway, visitors are presented with the subterranean workings of the prairie soil ecology on view for year round observation. While offering an interesting point of view on regional ecological education, the project fails to take advantage of the equally rich potential of revealing the subterranean realities of the site as an artificial construction. Remarkable for its rich and densely layered palette of landscape spaces, the Olin Partnership's project specified an absolutely diverse combination of sensory experiences and landscape typologies, including garden elements that represent Chicago's prominent cultural institutions. The project devotes individual gardens to the sensory pleasures of taste, the spatial gymnastics of landscape mazes, the visual effects of Impressionist painting, as well as the grass and sky of Chicago's wetland ecology. While absolutely convincing in its enthusiasm for the potential richness of landscape as a destination tourist site, the project is packed full with every event and experience imaginable, without offering anything new in terms of contemporary landscape design strategies and failing to acknowledge the artifice in their arrangement and commodification on this artificially constructed site.

The two projects removed from consideration last prior to the finalists were ranked as numbers four and five. Michael Van Valkenburgh of Cambridge, Massachusetts, authored the fourth ranked project, just missing the finalist round. This project resolved many of the subtler difficulties of the project including the orchestration of a larger site strategy for circulation while simultaneously providing a stunning array of densely planted floral displays throughout the year. While the jury praised its combination of elements across scales and its thorough presentation, it is a garden perhaps more suited to another site. Studio On Site of Tokyo submitted the fifth ranked project and the project most challenging to conventional notions of what a garden is and what it does. In their garden, Studio On Site proposed a series of clearly marked linear landscape strips running north-south across the site and serviced by a pair of overhead gantry cranes continuously available for the ongoing removal, installation, and maintenance of constantly changing curated installations of potted plant material. This remarkable proposal was the most daring in questioning the curious thinness of the site's construction as parking garage roof garden, while providing for the necessary seasonal change, floral displays, and solving the various circulation and spatial relationships surrounding the site. By doing away with the deceptively thin veneer of topsoil on top of the enormous three-story multi-use building below and invoking the direct technology of the train line itself in making of the project rather than its representation, the project presented a clear critique of conventional notions of landscape, offering a compelling vision of a post-modern nature gallery where installations are curated and installed in the same way works of art are arranged in the gallery to construct new readings, meanings, and conditions for future work.

Fig. 1. Gustafson Landscape: Esso Headquarters.
Fig. 2. Israel Performance. Fig. 3. Oudolf Planting: Winter.

LOUIS BENECH

MILLENNIUM GARDEN

WITH NEUTRALITY AND modesty of expression respectful of the rich architectural voices, this unifying space will be destined to enforce peaceful and safe privacy, calm, and serenity. The force of a single stream propagating the undulation of the elevated pathway across Columbus Drive will solely rupture the soft and uniform whisper.

The underlying structure, as the bird in flight can see, is reminiscent of the urban grid that nurtures adjacent street forms. From whatever approach (the best angle being from the tangent rising from Monroe Street) the visitor coming upon this parcel will discover a flowering prairie, a meadow voluntarily artificial in nature for it remains a garden on slab, nature itself is close, beautiful, and inspiring.

During the flowering season, the field will be covered with stars more numerous than that of the states. Like constellations, shrubs appear and provide structure to the winter landscape. Twelve trees from around the world punctuate the nebula. They speak of a diversity of cultures but state none in particular and are selected for their growth habit and the striking beauty of their bark. The triangulation of the sites of these trees matches the planets cartography in the Chicago sky on the first minute of January 1, 2001.

The formal discourse hereby embeds the date of entrance in this new era at the core of the garden and let the dreams and emotions take over and submerge the initial stimulus that composed this piece of landscape.

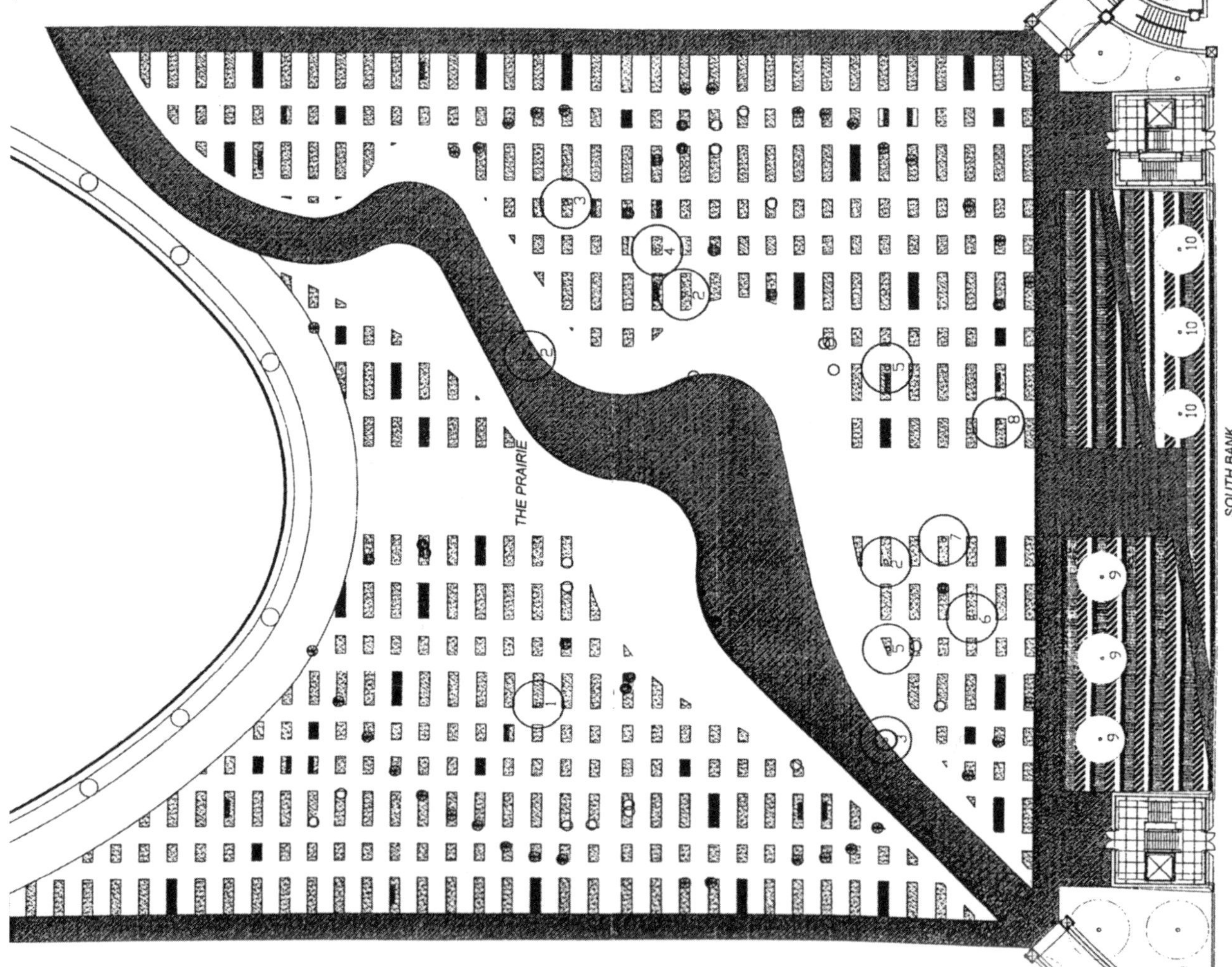

During the flowering season, the field will be covered with stars more numerous than that of the states. Like constellations, shrubs appear and provide structure to the winter landscape.

Fig. 1. Garden Plan.
Fig. 2. Perspective View Winter.

CLOCK HOUSE DENMANS
MILLENNIUM GARDEN

MY INITIAL REACTION on feeling the site potential was of being overwhelmed by the importance of the location, the disparity of building styles, and the scale and geometry of the surrounding tower blocks. I felt that with so much *prima donna* creativity around that the landscape needed a simple treatment, which should not only embody the scale of its surround, but also provide a human environment at all seasons. The human scale should be comfortable for both the individual as well as the crowd. Pattern was important to relate the hard landscape treatment to the scale of its surroundings, but the planting overlay was what would create an intimate park or garden feel.

I was very moved some time ago by visiting the studio of Frank Lloyd Wright. Chicago has meant Frank Lloyd Wright. It has something to do with the term Midwest, which has a romantic connotation strengthened by the patterns of farm layouts and prairies. The asymmetric geometry relating to the formality of the site, the profile of surrounding tower blocks, and the *Beaux-Arts* layout of the rest of the park influence the layout. The interplay of shape and structure defining outside space interests me.

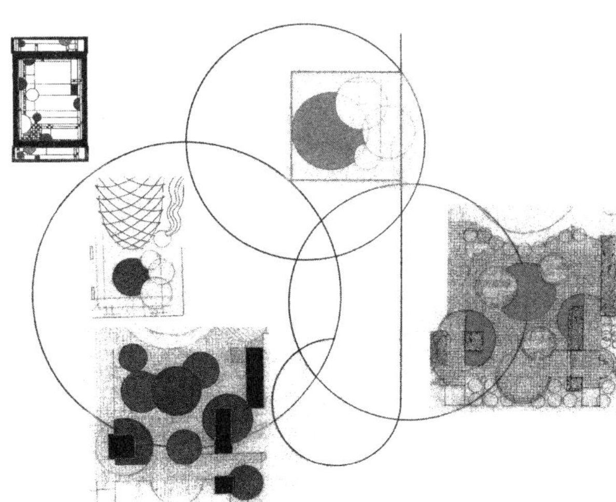

Fig. 1. Garden Plan. Fig. 2. Garden Diagram.

> Pattern was important to relate the hard landscape treatment to the scale of its surroundings, but the planting overlay was what would create an intimate park or garden feel.

GLASS GARDEN

WIND AND WATER GARDEN

OUR INSPIRATION WAS the wind and water, presences that so imbue the city of Chicago. To catch the wind, we chose grass. Beautiful drifts of colorful grasses that know hard winters, but return in full spring splendor. Low maintenance mass planting of just four kinds of ornamental grass (and their varieties) that grow green or blue in spring, blaze red and yellow in fall, then stand straight and gold through winter dormancy. Cut back in earliest spring, all these grasses will return with full vigor after little or no replanting.

To illustrate the water, we chose glass. Thick textured surfaces, safe in all weather, allow for a variety of lighting play. Everything is made entirely from recycled material: glass pavers on all the pathways, amber glass pylons to mark wide passages evoke the moorings of a harbor, a glass gravel *Meditation Garden* where pondering reveals surreal surprises, and frosted glass for "floating benches," large circular forms seemingly suspended in mid-space.

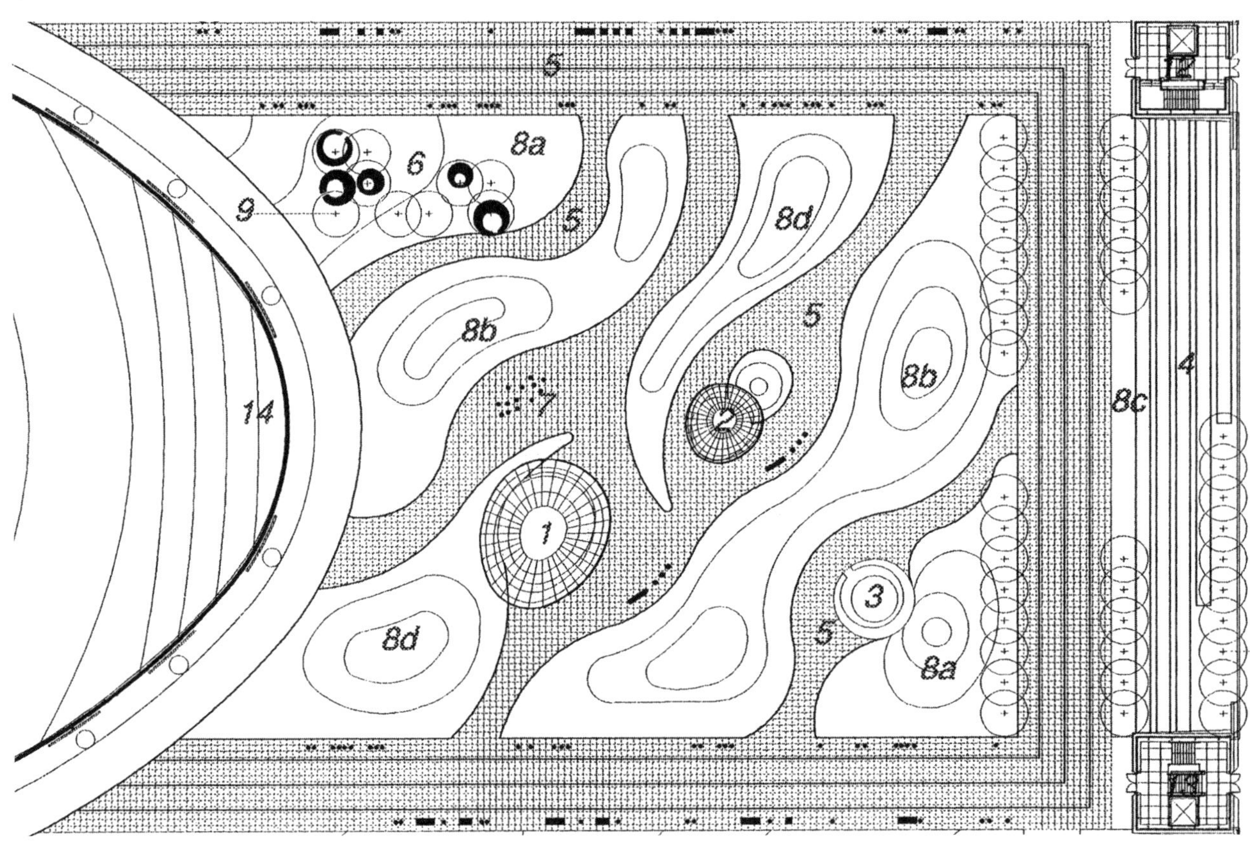

Low maintenance mass planting of just four kinds of ornamental grass (and their varieties) that grow green or blue in spring, blaze red and yellow in fall, then stand straight and gold through winter dormancy.

Fig. 1. Garden Plan.
Fig. 2. Perspective View Grass Field.

FOUR SEASONS GARDEN

WE LOOKED TO the grid implicit in Chicago's urban fabric of architecture and streets, and to the grid of the Midwest's agricultural landscape. *Four Seasons Garden* is configured in a classical cruciform shape, divided into smaller square "rooms" of two types: corner *Exuberant Gardens* and tailored *Pattern Gardens* situated at the four points of the compass. The energetic *Exuberant Gardens*, with their lush overflowing annuals, are filled with ever-changing seasonal displays. The juxtaposition of their "planned indifference" with *Pattern Gardens'* geometric formality illustrates the aesthetic play between nature's endless vitality and its shaping by human design.

Each of the four pattern "rooms" celebrates one of Chicago's distinct seasons. Within each of these spaces, four walkways converge at a centrally located water sculpture. These commissioned pieces function as fountains in season, and remain expressive artworks throughout the rest of the year. The works mounted on pedestals made of differing materials represent varying historical eras. Traditional *parterres* surround the fountains. However, providing a twist, the boxwood hedges are shaped into the stylized forms of leaves from trees indigenous to the

> The juxtaposition of "planned indifference" with the pattern gardens' geometric formality illustrates the aesthetic play between nature's endless vitality and its shaping by human design.

Midwest: Illinois' State Tree, the White Oak, and the Sumac made famous by the great architects of Chicago's Prairie School.

A comfortable sense of scale in these intimate inner "rooms" provides solace to visitors to *Four Seasons Garden*. Just steps from any of these rooms, visitors find themselves in a very different kind of space, *The Central Green*: a flat, simply patterned lawn, inlaid with granite tracery. The green is designed to offer visitors an enclosed level setting ideal for taking in the awe-inspiring view of Chicago's impressive skyline.

Fig. 1. Bird's-Eye View Looking North.
Fig. 2. Bird's-Eye View Exuberant Garden.

OLIN PARTNERSHIP

A GARDEN CELEBRATION OF CHICAGO

THIS GARDEN IS a celebration of Chicago culture and landscape. It is conceived as a collage of six interconnected gardens commemorating some of the cultural institutions for which the city is famous. These institutions nourish the body, mind, and spirit of its residents and visitors, and bring joy into the city's life. The magic of the garden is generated by its close proximity to the Lake, the Loop, and some of the city's outstanding institutions, as well as its views of the city skyline and Lake Michigan. Millennium Park, with this new garden, is another opportunity to attract people to this great city and, in the process, contribute to the creation of wonderful memories.

A Garden Celebration of Chicago is designed to contrast with the orthogonal formality of the larger context of Grant and Millennium Parks that surround it. The overall design structure incorporates a large central space composed of three subsidiary gardens. The subsidiary gardens, *Grass and Sky Garden*, *Jens Jensen "Prairie River" Aquatic Garden*, and *Prairie Garden*, represent the natural landscape of Chicago. The cultural landscape of today is represented by the gardens to the east and west: *Impressionist Garden*, *Taste of the World Garden*, and *Maze & Labyrinth Garden*.

Millennium Park, with this new garden, is another opportunity to attract people to this great city and, in the process, contribute to the creation of wonderful memories.

Fig. 1. Garden Plan.
Fig. 2. Perspective View.

STUDIO ON SITE

LIVING CHICAGO

LIVING CHICAGO UTILIZES technology in order to achieve a more human, natural, and memorable garden than we have known before. We propose a garden where humanity, technology, and environment co-exist. We present a garden for the next generations living in Chicago.

Chicago truly represents four different seasons. The garden will capture every moment of these changes, and it will present seasonal events and activities while delivering heartwarming natural gifts. The garden should reflect Chicagoan's lifestyles, and grow with their participation. People will enjoy visiting the garden where their own creations are accommodated. The garden not only reflects four seasonal changes, but also samples and preserves a part of the local ecosystem. Sampling a local environment and retaining it with minimum maintenance, the garden

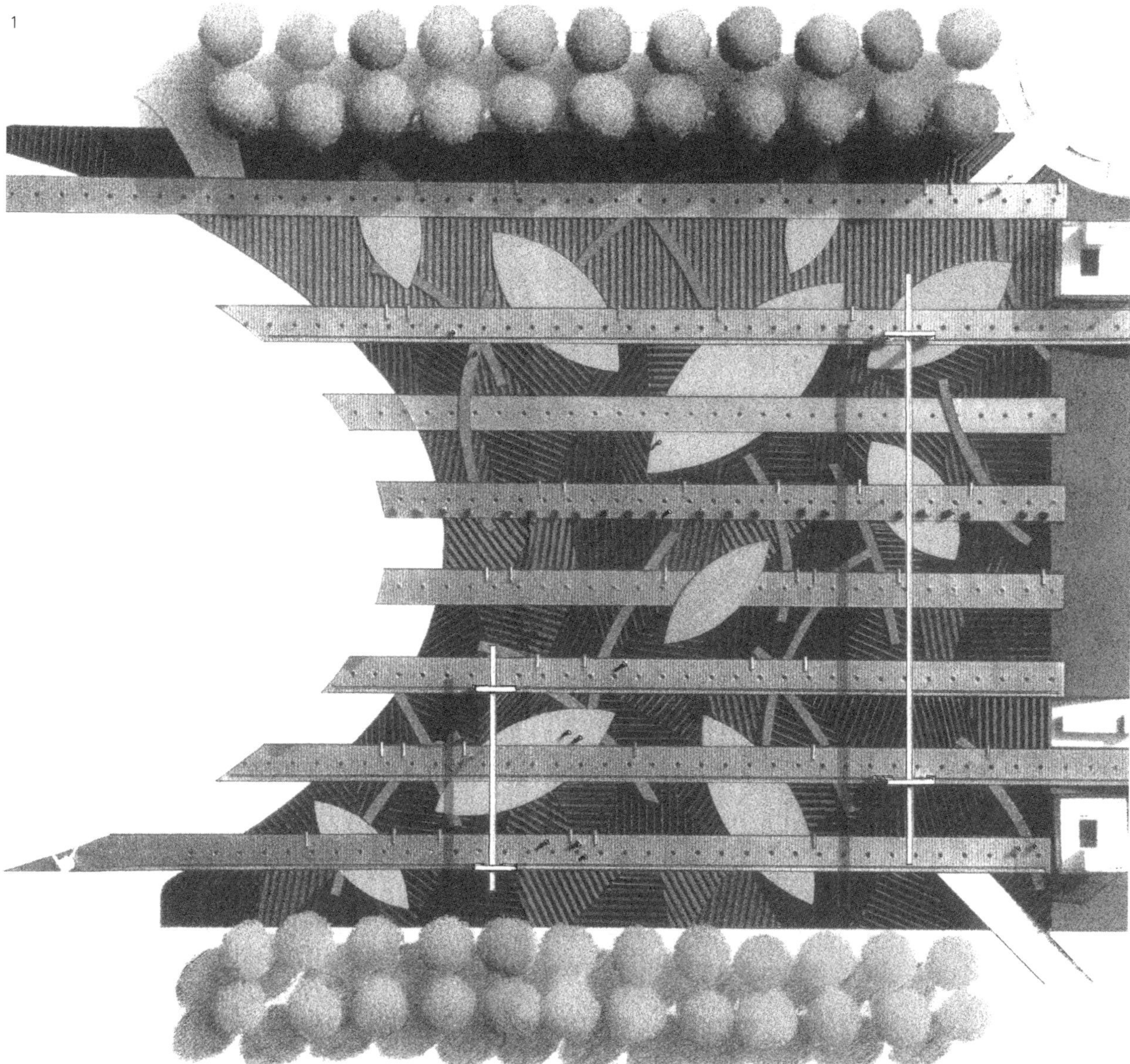

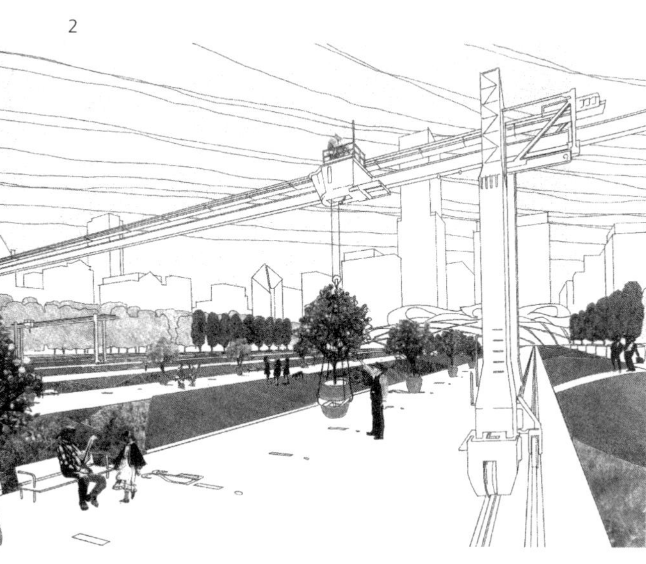

Fig. 1. Garden Plan. Fig. 2. Perspective View Crane.

> The Platform functions as a major pedestrian pathway, and is paved for heavy use. It incorporates the drainage system, lighting, signage, and garden furniture.

will educate people and raise interest in beauty and the importance of the surrounding environment.

The Green Yard is open to natural vegetation in the area, representing the local ecology. With a minimum of maintenance this yard will preserve the natural vegetation and will also accept invading species from other sites. *The Leaf Lawn* is a green open space where people can sit, gather, and rest. *The Platform* functions as a major pedestrian pathway, and is paved for heavy use. People can also watch the performing arts on the paved

Platform, which can also function as a stage. It incorporates the drainage system, lighting, signage, and garden furniture. The use of a large overhead crane resolves all maintenance issues like irrigation, plant maintenance, and cleaning, as well as seasonal potted plant and tree movement, by approaching from the sky. This "hyper-maintenance object" eliminates unnecessarily large garden passages for maintenance, and brings back cozy human-scaled public space.

Fig. 1. North-South Garden Section.

WE BELIEVE IN the transformative power of landscape. We want this garden to feel like no other place in Chicago: indeterminate in depth, visually active and complex, and dominated by an overflowing abundance of plants.

At the center of the garden, planting occurs on circular landforms, which will be six to seven feet in height when the herbaceous plants are in bloom. These sensual forms will create a welcoming feeling, and will complement, by contrast, the linearity of the rest of Millennium Park and the grid of Chicago. Half of the planted islands will have flowering trees, and the other half will be open to the sun. With herbaceous plantings rising to eye level and flowering trees arching over the walks, the experience will be like Monet's tunnels of flowers at Giverny.

Surrounding the inner garden, an area of larger landforms and broader pedestrian areas will absorb and engage the crowds surging through the garden before and after concerts. The intention is a public landscape of abundance and sensuality.

As an enveloping spatial frame, the entire garden is encircled in plantings of Golden Weeping Willows. The willows' soft textures, their dreamlike forms, and their beguiling winter habit will transport the garden's visitors, engaging their feelings and imaginations and creating an expansive place of psychological immensity.

> The primary goal of this design has been to evolve the right combination of spaces, landforms, walking corridors, and planted areas to honor plants as a design medium.

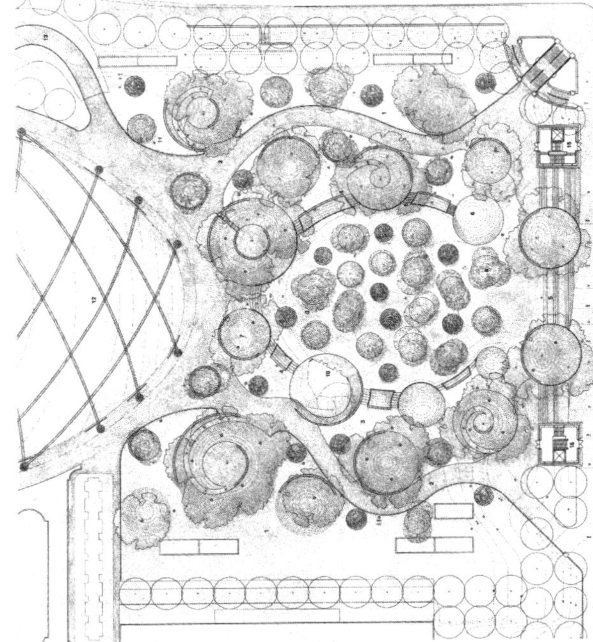

Fig. 2. Garden Plan.

PETER WALKER AND PARTNERS
THE GLASS PRAIRIE

THE AGRICULTURAL PRODUCTS of the prairie lie at the heart of Chicago's identity. Chicago was created at the margin of a lake and surrounded by a landscape far different from the ones encountered by pioneers in the east. The boundless spaces that spoke of the endless opportunities made Chicago a great urban center of railroads and trade. And yet spacious prairie landscape is no longer available to visitors to Grant Park in its visible presence, or in its emotional meaning. It is more remote from their experience than the most exotic of horticultural displays.

With this indigenous and fundamental, yet largely invisible landscape in mind, we propose *The Glass Prairie* as a new garden in Millennium Park, a garden that reveals both the visual and the poetic truth of the grounding of the city of Chicago. *The Glass Prairie* is the re-created prairie landscape of a glacial kame in northeastern Illinois. A circle, 165 feet in diameter, comprising half an acre, and slightly mounded to a height of six feet, it is bounded by a wooden seatwall and divided into quarters by two intersecting glass-walled paths, which are twenty feet wide and floored in stainless steel. As the paths pass through the mound, the inner workings of the prairie are revealed through the five by ten feet panels of the glass walls. Visible there is the soil in the composition and depth appropriate to each zone of the kame. This is living soil, home to the billions of invisible microorganisms that constitute fertile soil.

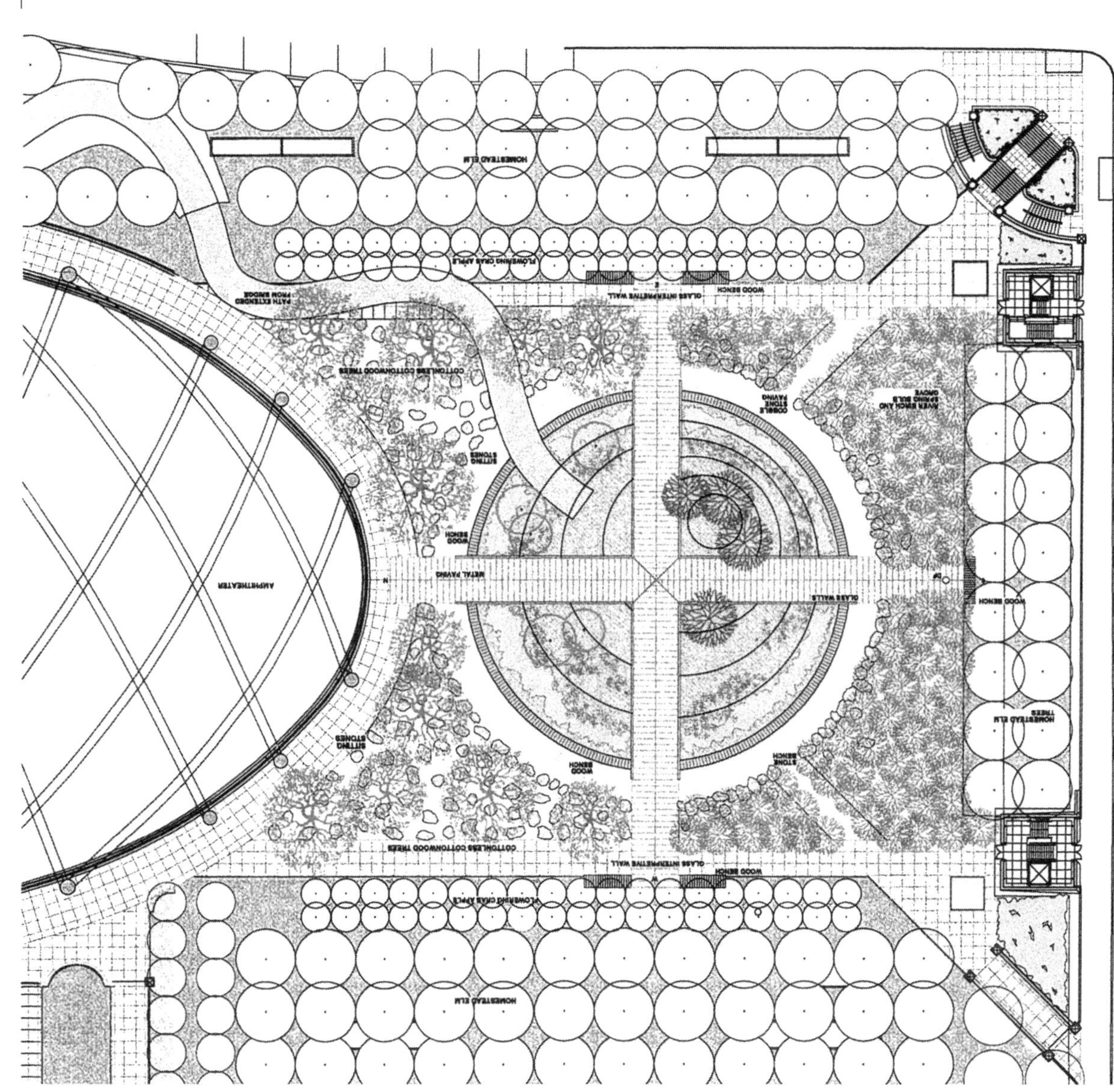

As the paths pass through the mound, the inner workings of the prairie are revealed through the five feet by ten feet panels of the glass walls.

Fig. 1. Garden Plan.
Fig. 2. Garden Section Prairie Mound.

PROJECT CREDITS

KATHRYN GUSTAFSON PARTNERS
(Seattle, Washington and London, England)
PIET OUDOLF (Hummelo, Netherlands)
ROBERT ISRAEL (Los Angeles, California)
The Shoulder Garden

    Kathryn Gustafson, principal
    Piet Oudolf, principal
    Robert Israel, principal
    Shannon Nichol, project designer
    Jennifer Guthrie, project manager
    Alan McWain, designer
    Rodrigo Abela, designer
    Gareth Loveridge, designer
    Rauda Scale Models, modelmaker

OFFICE OF DAN KILEY
(Charlotte, Vermont)
Millennium Garden

    Dan Kiley, principal
    Peter Meyer
    Nanda Patel

JEFF MENDOZA GARDEN
(New York, New York)
Urban Riff Garden

    Jeff Mendoza, principal
    Robert Monteleone
    Signe Nielson, Signe Nielsen Landscape

LOUIS BENECH
(Paris, France)
Millennium Garden

    Louis Benech, principal

CLOCK HOUSE DENMANS
(West Sussex, England)
Millennium Garden

    John Brookes, principal
    Catherine Fallon, assistant
    Clive Mercer Associates

GLASS GARDEN
(Los Angeles, California)
Wind and Water Garden

    Andy Cao, principal
    Stephen Jerrom, principal
    Mathew Randolph, landscape architect
    Kiku Kurahashi, landscape architect
    Amy Korn, landscape architect
    Nancy Bearnth, computer graphics

DOUGLAS HOERR
(Evanston, Illinois)
Four Seasons Garden

    Douglas Hoerr, principal designer
    Claire Kettelkamp, project manager
    Ryan Kettelkamp, project manager
    David Lawrie, project manager
    Kathleen Golumb, project manager
    Tiffany Steffen, landscape architect
    William Heidbreder, landscape architect
    Emily Placke, landscape architect
    Ron Taylor, artist
    Tracy Taylor, graphic designer
    Maren Nelson, writer
    Yvonne Smith, writer

OLIN PARTNERSHIP
(Philadelphia, Pennsylvania)
A Garden Celebration of Chicago

    Dennis C. McGlade, partner-in-charge
    Howard Supnik, associate
    David Elliot, senior landscape architect
    Frank Garnier, director of graphic design
    Annie Griffenberg, landscape designer
    Lori Johnson, graphic designer
    Matt Plecity, landscape architect
    Samantha Schweitzer, senior landscape designer
    Linda Walczak, senior landscape designer

STUDIO ON SITE
(Tokyo, Japan)
Living Chicago

    Hiroki Hasegawa
    Toru Mitani
    Chisa Toda
    Toshio Tsushima
    Chiho Suzuki

MICHAEL VAN VALKENBURGH ASSOCIATES
(Cambridge, Massachusetts)
Four Seasons Garden

    Michael Van Valkenburgh, principal
    Mathew Urbanski
    Kristan First
    Jane Choi
    Samir Khanna
    Soheyung Kim
    William Madden
    Jen Pindyck

PETER WALKER AND PARTNERS
(Berkeley, California)
The Glass Prairie

    Peter Walker, principal
    Jane Gillette
    James Haig Streeter
    Paul Sieron
    Christopher Grubbs, illustrations
    Steven Apfelbaum, Applied Ecological Services

ILLUSTRATION CREDITS

COVER
Courtesy Gustafson Partners.

TITLE PAGE
Courtesy Gustafson Partners.

PAGES VIII-IX
Fig. 1.   Courtesy Piet Oudolf.
Fig. 2.   Courtesy Robert Israel.
Fig. 3.   Courtesy Gustafson Partners / Claire De Virieu.

PAGES X-XI
Fig. 1.   Courtesy Piet Oudolf.
Fig. 2.   Courtesy Gustafson Partners.
Fig. 3.   Courtesy Robert Israel.

PAGES XII-1
Fig. 1.   Courtesy Piet Oudolf.
Fig. 2.   Courtesy Robert Israel.
Fig. 3.   Courtesy Gustafson Partners.

PAGES 2-3
Fig. 1.   Courtesy Piet Oudolf.
Fig. 2.   Courtesy Gustafson Partners.
Fig. 3.   Courtesy Robert Israel.
Fig. 4.   Courtesy Lawrence Okrent.

PAGES 4-5
Fig. 1.   Courtesy Gary Taber.
Fig. 2.   Courtesy Gary Taber.
Fig. 3.   Courtesy Millennium Park.

PAGES 6-7
Fig. 1.   Courtesy Piet Oudolf.
Fig. 2.   Courtesy Gustafson Partners.
Fig. 3.   Courtesy Robert Israel.
Fig. 4.   Courtesy Chicago Historical Society.
Fig. 5.   Courtesy Chicago Historical Society.

PAGES 8-9
Fig. 1.   Courtesy Chicago Historical Society.
Fig. 2.   Courtesy Chicago Historical Society.
Fig. 3.   Courtesy Chicago Parks District Special Collections.
Fig. 4.   Courtesy Skidmore, Owings and Merrill.
Fig. 5.   Courtesy Chicago Parks District Special Collections.

PAGES 10-11
Fig. 1.   Courtesy Piet Oudolf.
Fig. 2.   Courtesy Gustafson Partners.
Fig. 3.   Courtesy Robert Israel.
Fig. 4.   Courtesy Lawrence Okrent.

PAGES 12-13
Figs. 1-3.   Courtesy Frank O. Gehry Associates.
Fig. 4.   Courtesy Anish Kapoor.

PAGES 14-15
Fig. 1.   Courtesy Piet Oudolf.
Fig. 2.   Courtesy Gustafson Partners.
Fig. 3.   Courtesy Robert Israel.
Fig. 4.   Courtesy Gustafson Partners.

PAGES 16-17
Figs. 1-4.   Courtesy Gustafson Partners.

PAGES 18-19
Figs. 1-4.   Courtesy Gustafson Partners.

PAGES 20-21
Figs. 1-4.   Courtesy Gustafson Partners.

PAGES 22-23
Figs. 1-4.   Courtesy Gustafson Partners.

PAGES 24-25
Fig. 1.   Courtesy Piet Oudolf.
Fig. 2.   Courtesy Gustafson Partners.
Fig. 3.   Courtesy Robert Israel.

PAGES 26-27
Figs. 1-5.   Courtesy Office of Dan Kiley.

PAGES 28-29
Figs. 1-5.   Courtesy Jeff Mendoza Garden.

PAGES 30-31
Fig. 1.   Courtesy Gustafson Partners.
Fig. 2.   Courtesy Robert Israel.
Fig. 3.   Courtesy Piet Oudolf.

PAGE 32
Figs. 1-2.   Courtesy Louis Benech.

PAGE 33
Figs. 1-2.   Courtesy Clock House Denmans.

PAGE 34
Figs. 1-2.   Courtesy Glass Garden.

PAGE 35
Figs. 1-2.   Courtesy Douglas Hoerr.

PAGE 36
Figs. 1-2.   Courtesy Olin Partnership.

PAGE 37
Figs. 1-2.   Courtesy Studio on Site.

PAGE 38
Figs. 1-2.   Courtesy Michael Van Valkenburgh Associates.

PAGE 39
Figs. 1-2.   Courtesy Peter Walker and Partners.

CHICAGO CULTURAL CENTER

78 East Washington Street
Chicago, Illinois 60602

312.744.6630

www.cityofchicago.org/Tour/CulturalCenter/

Department of Cultural Affairs
City of Chicago, Richard M. Daley, Mayor

University of Illinois Press / Urbana and Chicago

The publication of *Constructed Ground* has been generously supported by:

RICHARD H. DRIEHAUS FOUNDATION
SARA LEE CORPORATION
MILLENNIUM PARK INCORPORATED
GEORGIA-PACIFIC CORPORATION

PAPER: GEORGIA-PACIFIC CORPORATION, TITANIUM™ OPAQUE
DESIGN: HENNESSY DESIGN GROUP, INC.